ANDREW SEARS

UN BOOK

The 30 Commandments of Human Agreement

BALBOA.
PRESS

A DIVISION OF HAY HOUSE

Balboa Press books may be ordered through booksellers or by contacting:

Balboa Press
A Division of Hay House
1663 Liberty Drive
Bloomington, IN 47403
www.balboapress.com
1 (877) 407-4847

Because of the dynamic nature of the Internet, any web addresses or links contained in
this book may have changed since publication and may no longer be valid. The views
expressed in this work are solely those of the author and do not necessarily reflect the views
of the publisher, and the publisher hereby disclaims any responsibility for them.

The author of this book does not dispense medical advice or prescribe the use of any technique as a form
of treatment for physical, emotional, or medical problems without the advice of a physician, either directly
or indirectly. The intent of the author is only to offer information of a general nature to help you in your quest
for emotional and spiritual well-being. In the event you use any of the information in this book for yourself,
which is your constitutional right, the author and the publisher assume no responsibility for your actions.

Any people depicted in stock imagery provided by Getty Images are models,
and such images are being used for illustrative purposes only.
Certain stock imagery © Getty Images.

Scripture quotations are from The Holy Bible, English Standard Version® (ESV®), copyright © 2001 by
Crossway, a publishing ministry of Good News Publishers. Used by permission. All rights reserved.

This book is a work of non-fiction. Unless otherwise noted, the author and the publisher make
no explicit guarantees as to the accuracy of the information contained in this book and in
some cases, names of people and places have been altered to protect their privacy.

ISBN: 978-1-5043-9974-6 (sc)
ISBN: 978-1-5043-9975-3 (e)

Print information available on the last page.

Balboa Press rev. date: 04/09/2018

Contents

Dedication

Aiden: a rockstar, thank you for the book cover idea to decorate the book in flags
Jim: a strong man in the Kingdom of Heaven, who teaches
through example the meaning of Christian love.
Michael: always available to talk to and to converge on my prayers
and ideas. You really helped this book take shape.
Dad: Thank you for supporting this work to the finish line, you
are a great Dad and gave this book new breathe.

Introduction

UN Book

The 30 Commandments
United Nations, charter for Declaration of Human Rights

Interpretations:

Ok so William Penn was called by Ben Franklin, the best lawmaker ever. I concur that William Penn was very good at what he focused into being, and made major contributions to our country. I think laws are reserved for God, and the universal postulates. What we share are agreements, so I don't consider myself a lawyer but a higher octave agreementmaker. So William Penn was the greatest at making laws, and I am inspired by William Penn, and like him I am a very good and well studied agreement maker.

You don't need to go to law school to understand about what Donald Trump calls, "The Art of the Deal" which is the social roles that bring forth our agreements for society. So there is something that many people do not know about, and that is the wonderful work done after World War II, under the leadership of Eleanor Roosevelt, to form a human rights charter under the United Nations. These I will politely call, with respect to religious tradition, the 30 commandments that reign supreme over all other jurisdictions of United Nations Member States.

To interpret law, is something that requires a lot of sophistication, and I do think in a system of order my interpretations are superior to what is currently in practice. As Jesus said, "new wine is meant for a new glass", and I hope to reflect society under the values of the United Nations, and the standing agreement as it's been, as a bigger fish than the United States constitution in all American law, and there is very good reason for that to be so. I will do extrapolations and interpretations of the central and nexus document, of the virtue of human rights, and what values actually are at the center of the law, or jurisdictional agreements.

I would like the reader to print their own copy of the United Nations charter on the Universal Declaration of Human Rights penned in 1948. I want the reader to begin to study these for themselves and ponder the values of society. You can find it at the UN website, at the link http://www.un.org/en/universal-declaration-human-rights/. In the back of this book is a copy of the full Declaration of Human Rights and a customization for you to write your own interpretations on each article. I am going to reflect this very important document in great and living color in my interpretations. I will qualify my interpretations so you will see where they derive from. The Human Rights Charter begins with a Preamble, and then contains 30 articles on the values of human rights. This document should be a pattern for the great agreementmakers of tomorrow.

Preamble

Whereas recognition of the inherent dignity and of the equal and inalienable rights of all members of the human family is the foundation of freedom, justice and peace in the world,

Whereas disregard and contempt for human rights have resulted in barbarous acts which have outraged the conscience of mankind, and the advent of a world in which human beings shall enjoy freedom of speech and belief and freedom from fear and want has been proclaimed as the highest aspiration of the common people,

Whereas it is essential, if man is not to be compelled to have recourse, as a last resort, to rebellion against tyranny and oppression, that human rights should be protected by the rule of law,

Whereas it is essential to promote the development of friendly relations between nations,

Whereas the peoples of the United Nations have in the Charter reaffirmed their faith in fundamental human rights, in the dignity and worth of the human person and in the equal rights of men and women and have determined to promote social progress and better standards of life in larger freedom,

Whereas Member States have pledged themselves to achieve, in co-operation with the United Nations, the promotion of universal respect for and observance of human rights and fundamental freedoms,

Whereas a common understanding of these rights and freedoms is of the greatest importance for the full realization of this pledge,

Now, Therefore THE GENERAL ASSEMBLY proclaims THIS UNIVERSAL DECLARATION OF HUMAN RIGHTS as a common standard of achievement for all peoples and all nations, to the end that every individual and every organ of society, keeping this Declaration constantly in mind, shall strive by teaching and education to promote respect for these rights and freedoms and by progressive measures, national and international, to secure their universal and effective recognition and observance, both among the peoples of Member States themselves and among the peoples of territories under their jurisdiction.

Preamble:

Read the Universal Declaration of Human Rights Preamble. Meditate on it, try to commit it to memory, and ask yourself what the implications are. Remember after WWII, certain states decided to join together to prevent human rights violations that happened in and around Germany, and our collective asking grew so much that we came to an agreement. This is the document that helped us past that chapter, and a light truly went up so that if we honor our agreement, with the virtue of human rights values reigning supreme, we would not do that to each other any more. And if we have to have humility before natural disasters, we don't have to tear down each other. This is a very, very high virtue that is above racism, above homophobia, above xenophobia, above ethnocentrism, and to get to that point is a personal climb. In our immaturity we cling to other values, and the climb will eventually get us to see the light at the end of the tunnel. Not everybody who goes into positions of authority is in touch with the big picture. You should know that United Nations resonance, came from an evolutionary leap, where we found a higher octave above nationalism. A plateau was reached that will forever be a flag in history. There will be few in the generations waning, who will see and initiate into their offspring, virtues that have obviously no virtue but in its undoing. This United Nations resonance is a very good refuge from chaos and the writings are very virtuous.

The Human Rights charter is a pledge that many major jurisdictions including the United States have consented to. To sign up for the United Nations, is a choice made by certain nations. Not every country is a part of the United Nations. As the United States of America is sovereign over many states including Pennsylvania, the United Nations is a larger law and agreement then the President of United States, and the two other branches of government. This is something that I know for sure. I interpret all law with the same fervor, and the member states who consented to the United Nations contract, which is most of the developed world share this as a central and nexus contract to all law agreement. So even though it has been obscure, this document is far superior in virtue and importance than the readily known "Bill of Rights" or the full United States constitution, or any constitution of the 50 states

So what does it mean, that all member states have taken the pledge of the promotion of human rights in the fullest realization? It should be in any court, the highest of virtue towards promoting "social progress." Now what does social progress mean, it means that this is a living document in one sense, but full of protection by it's non-distinction. For example, human rights are without variety. But Civil Rights take many forms and shapes throughout history, in our past century in America we waged the liberation of women's rights, race rights, sexual identity rights, gender identity rights, and the social progress is the realization to know that there is more Civil Rights to come, and to know how to recognize the movement early, and their needs, so we don't hurt a lot of people in the process.

The preamble talks about man being compelled to have recourse if the government is an oppressor, which does happen all the time throughout history as man is flawed. In the Hebrew tradition the letter "R" was used to mean the "evil inclination" and the reason that is, is all decisions are made with lack of knowledge of the whole picture. We do want to promote not the values of a treason happy paranoia, as if a president or leader presents a nationalistic agenda that is regressive, he will get many of his people to spin in those eddies, but he does not share the virtue of the United Nations which has a more expanded consciousness. This is contrary to popular opinion. Our leaders and our laws should not reflect by the very laws that govern our whole system, an isolationism that breaks connection with the global family. People may spin in those eddies today, because there is really no presentation or promotion of Human Rights as the highest expression of the law. As a result it is important to note, just because someone talks loud, does not mean their words holds any weight. Now what we do share as Member states, is this human rights declaration document, and your right to recourse against tyranny and oppression.

But here is the thing. This should not be a strange island that the respecter and honorer of human rights is a minority. Every expression of United States, Federal and State constitutions and agreements, should be under the virtue of expressing the Human Rights pledge in its fullest realization. This should not be only on the citizen but on the hierarchy of the courts to reflect and I'm hoping with this document promotion and awareness of these 30 commandments becomes something very common place. No expression of the laws should ever virtue the open invitation to bigotry, by those who go into positions of power seeking to discriminate in their own darkness, without oversight of higher virtue.

We can get rid of bigotry very easily, and that is through an alchemical transmutation of belief systems. Jesus taught, "he who is first will be last, and last will be first." On that note, I want to talk about Charles Manson, as he was my example growing up of a "bad guy" who called out violence on many lives. I would like to add to this conversation that more violence was carried out by the Presidents in my lifetime. So when looking for a bad guy, we need to know that it is a very false construct. At the same time lets add in violence carried out directly by Biblical avatars Moses, David, and Paul. So when we say the name Charles Manson, we can not separate him from the eternal brotherhood of all men. From our sins we can see that human is capable of great error. Some we consider heroes and some we consider villains. We need to learn that the bad guy is a false construct and will not serve the emerging paradigm.

So the common understanding of these 30 commandments is paramount to equality, and also promotion of a world of human rights. I will from time to time come back to the preamble, as I built in my understanding and grow I hope these meditations on the 30 articles can bring great gains in the virtues of human rights in America and around the world. We should then teach these 30 golden commandments as paramount to our whole political structure.

Article 1

All human beings are born free and equal in dignity and rights. They are endowed with reason and conscience and should act towards one another in a spirit of brotherhood.

Please read the declaration article for yourself. At this point it introduces the word "all" to mean each and every person, in a gestalt sense, and without exception. We are born free. We are born equal. These are words of the agreement that should be treasured in the hearts of all who are a part of this American experiment. What we all share, all of us human beings, is that we have dignity. And we have rights, that are spelled out in these articles. Now we are endowed with both reason and conscience. What is beautiful to me about the charter is that it originated in the English language, not a Bible scramble back through the Greek, Aramaic, and Hebrew languages so you are reading the direct translation. We all have dignity and rights, what do they mean to you? And each of us are endowed with reason and conscience. These are very wonderful things to have, to have the ability as individuals to reason and to have conscience. And in our constitutions and agreementlaws, we are to act towards one another with the virtue of brotherhood.

Jesus said, "If you have anything against your brother, leave your gift at the altar, and reconcile your brother." This is very huge. In what I call the foundations of each jurisdiction, are the places where the least among us live. This includes in the justice systems, prisons, in the military, and other military like programs, where human rights within the jurisdiction are shrouded in its own secret location. In these foundations of each jurisdiction, including federal manifestations on state property, a whole group of people can go unchecked and human rights overlooked to the extent we should say, there are some places that look as if nobody ever tried. In a church, if someone gets in trouble, they pray for them. They pray and they very falsely trust the system that their government operates to handle the troubled person. Our prayers should require researching into these foundations and taking a role in seeing our prayers through. And all over the world, even in America, we have to go with the assumption that nobody of integrity has ever tried to implement human rights in these directions.

In the Foundations, there is a limited consciousness of higher virtue, and to see the spirit of brotherhood among all people as the highest virtue is something that will be new to many. It is not my position to remove people from their jobs in their Foundation mindsets, but to retrain them towards the higher virtue. It is not my position to put responsibility on any individual, but rather the quality of the localized social system.

To see each person treated with dignity, and conscience is something to put in the "new glass" and just begin to assume the positive manifestation that each person, who is under jurisdiction of a member State of the United Nations, has these rights. Our conscience does serve us, I see as hearing from the Holy Spirit, to dictate conscience in an individual.

Article 2

Everyone is entitled to all rights and freedoms set forth in this Declaration, without distinction of any kind, such as race, colour, sex, language, religion, political or other opinion, national or social origin, property, birth or other status.

Furthermore, no distinction shall be made on the basis of the political, jurisdictional or international status of the country or territory to which a person belongs, whether it be independent, trust, non-self-governing or under any other limitation of sovereignty.

Each article builds on the others, so please I encourage you to read and study the 2nd article before reading my commentary. There is something very special about article 2 and that it is blind to any distinction passed human. Many will say you have to acknowledge certain groups, or certain factions, certain races, in order for them to get out of the position of minority. To this I agree that causes are important to be expressed and that is for the 2nd tier called "Civil Rights." What is so good about non-distinction, is that each human does have equality irregardless of their body, or their beliefs, their sexuality, their tongue, or their ethnicity or any other category.

I listed a few categories of secondary "Civil Rights" which are very important. It is from all I can see, a larger protection of human rights, to hold equality whether they are red, brown, yellow, black, or white. There is a word that gets you into the club here on our beautiful earth, and that word is "human." All my adult life I have been understanding "us" as and through the expression of the church of being eternal. Eternal is very beautiful membership, and a more exclusive membership is to use the moniker of "human." That is something that we all share. To Led Zeppelin and their song Stairway to Heaven, this could be the word that "she" could use to get anything she came for. I'm very happy that we can use the word human and also "without distinction" as a staple in our understanding of agreements of our social systems.

There is no distinction of land or jurisdiction in determining the equality of humans. Now this is true of all who are human. It is the member States who are consenting to the need for concept of the human rights charter. Each human on planet Earth is what is meant by human, not just the member States. However only Member States are under the jurisdiction of the UN Human Rights Declaration. Now how does that work? All sovereign nations are eligible to join, it is only those who are ready, do they join by choice and consent to the agreement. We would like all the nations to join this club.

Article 3

Everyone has the right to life, liberty, and security of person.

Please read article 3 before giving ear to my interpretations. Article 3 is that everyone has a right to life. Which is a very huge deal, and though it is controversial, this to me is especial to the unborn. To the being who has been given life, this is something that God ordained, through the union of two becoming one, and it should be for us to make sure each baby coming in has the best life they can. I understand that I step on ants, and I do aim very highly not to be hypocritical in an area I know not of. I have great compassion on all who make these decisions, but I do try to excel in not only human but also animal rights. I hope that qualifies my pro life position. Also when a doctor will work on a mother, under the legal agreement, he has 2 patients. I see this as a very important thing. Would you want the opportunity at life?

This should mean the ability to make decisions in life on your own terms is in alignment with this as well. This is meant for the older crowd, when you are young you have great life and you should make every effort to be the change in the world you want, and we as your fellow humanship we should make sure for each individual that we are providing a social structure suitable for you. It is just us. There is nobody else. Jesus said, "all judgment on earth is granted to (the archetype of) the Son." If life becomes difficult, we need to let people know that the shoe is not just on their foot. To those with medical ailments, it should be on us to set our focus to reeling in the hows and whys of solving such ailments. And decisions a person wishes to make about their life should be on their terms.

Now each person is granted through Article 3 the right to liberty. Now liberty goes back to the idea of reason and conscience. Liberty over your own life very much reflects our understanding of property rights. When you are using your liberty in a public place you are not in transgression. When you cross another person's property then you have transgressed. This is a very huge foundation for interpreting the charter. With liberty you can begin a major conversation. You cannot coerce another human being, or you have now transgressed their liberty. Where do you draw the line on this and what still is liberty?

Liberty means that you have the right to your life, and your possessions, and what you do in your social life, provided that you do not hurt or transgress another. I will tell you the word liberty does not make such a clear distinction of where the line itself is on what is liberty of one, and where that liberty stops. The answer is that it doesn't stop, and this surprises people. You have the liberty under the law to the fullness of what you want to do and express yourself as a person. Only when you transgress against another, you in many ways do not break or ever hopefully lose your liberty but you have transgressed against the liberty of another. Liberty in life is extensive. While you have your life, and your reason, and your conscience, you have a very natural and supportive springboard to get you to the full life of liberty.

Now let's say somebodies social liberties alienate another person. If it is in a public place, and there is no physical intent to hurt another, and there are no health problems affecting another, then it is the liberty of the alienated to leave or use diplomacy to express their opinion. We don't need this to be a conversation of running out of space, people with different lifestyles can spread out in the world. If it is influence that is the thing that alienates, we all have equality as humans, and we all can influence others with equality. This is a huge conversation about what liberty is, because as people catch the implications there is a different paradigm when people start to understand the meaning of the word. What is your definition of liberty?

Now you also have security of person as a right, which now is the other side of liberty. You have the right to be protected from others who are out with intent to hurt you. Now there are many things that security of person contains, as we'll read later it is certain rights to social security, food, water, clothing, and shelter among many others. So not only do you have protection to those who transgress your human rights, you have the protection of person that is to make sure in collaboration with you, with resources of jurisdiction on up to the United Nations, that you have everything that is necessary for a healthy and productive life.

So when you value your rights as human, and your rights to life, liberty, and security of persons you want to extend that to those who would transgress you. As Jesus said to forgive, ("70x7") and "turn the other cheek." The real mark of this human right does come when you are able to view transgressors from the lens of their human rights, and our collective allowance of liberty. Do not look to focus on the transgressions, but rather focus on the human rights. I do believe that the great majority of transgressions will disappear by lack of market around them. That is something we have to acknowledge, is we have to ask our selves what and who are profiting from the lack of liberty, in all its many faces of discrimination, hatred, oppression and all those stepsisters.

Article 4

No one shall be held in slavery or servitude; slavery and the slave trade shall be prohibited in all their forms.

Please read article 4. Nobody shall be held in slavery or servitude. We did come a long way in the United States to surmount a great deal of slavery over the past century but a whole lot still remains. There was a man who lived at the time of Lincoln, named TW Stead, who was a very fascinating man, he was a writer, who met his demise on the Titanic. Through his articles he would speak out against the "white slave trade" which was the selling of young girls. He tried to make a point how easy it was to buy a girl to write in his publication, but he ended up getting arrested for his political stunt, of course meaning no harm to the girl. An outcry went up because of this, and as a result the Age of Consent which was at its highest 12 years old around the world, rose in the 1860s from 12 to 13, and then to 16 as an outcry to the white slave trade.

This was not an effective but very damaging thing for all people. Everybody growing up has had to deal with pushing this boulder up a hill whether they came to be proud in it, or wonder why it is that way. It seems still to this day that the idea of slavery is what the collective conscious wants to purge itself of while keeping liberty. And it does encroach on liberty in many forms in its overreach of that noble virtue. If you are principled to what liberty is, and you set your emotions to the beliefs of these principles, you're going to have to sort through a lot of leaven in the bread.

We still in our foundations, of the military, and the police, and the prisons, and all things like that hold people, humans, in slavery and servitude no less worse or absolute then any time in history. Our liberty definitions work here. If a person does consent to work, then by our economic system, they are following in human rights as it is a non-issue. When someone forces you to do something then that is a form of servitude, and this is a violation of personal liberty. Why? Because someone coerced another person, and took part of their security of person away. So we do in human rights conversation want a system based on the merits of consent, and only by that guide, can we focus in on the transgressions of liberty, and systematically bring these things to the light, and also those perpetrating the overreach of liberty.

Article 5

No one shall be subjected to torture or to cruel, inhuman or degrading treatment or punishment.

Please read article 5, for the blessing of all our posterity. These are my interpretations. Article 5 says that no one shall be subject to torture or to cruel, inhumane or degrading treatment or punishment. I will point out that this first of all is a negative command, and I do like positive commands, however this is something we can all point to and highlight to make sure that every inch of this world is humane. The major importance of article 5 is that it is without condition, as some others use the word "arbitrary" to make exceptions.

By consent of the charter, as a higher responsibility to nations above our own American constitution, this is the agreementlaw of the land. It is very important that they do use these words. Torture is a bad word, and I do like to liberate language, and for some language it's liberation is for distinction in progressing the cause of human and civil rights. There is no clause to say in the case of war that there is an exception to this. I don't know a correct definition on torture, I just know that it is something that we don't want in our world, and we should use our conscience, and reason to know that this is illegal to the highest of international law and any social system should embrace the viewpoint that there is no clause to creating torture.

Much of torture extends to the part of a person, the body that they are in that I believe in my own conviction that "inalienable" is the part of the body that a person can not escape. Sexual orientation and gender identity are a very big part of the inalienable rights and to try to change a person out of the part of them that was inalienable since their birth, and extends back into their gestation period, starting at the loving conception of mother and father, is a silent torture. To isolate a person in the room alone without any human contact, is another form of torture. Isolation is a very sad thing that is just as much torture as any other form of torture. Lack of caring is torture. If you have to question if it is torture, first of all don't do it, and yes it is torture. That should be the blueprint, if you have to ask the question, then you know that is torture. I will not highlight torture but only to say human nature can be very depraved, and all humans have access to redemption.

Cruelty is expressed in many ways. You have to start with the foundations. You may know that part of the natzi tragedy was gas chambers. What kind of cruel, and barbaric people would gas people in a room without air? Turns out, the United States, portrays in its very own army training video that they gas the new recruits. Just as cruel as putting all those people in the chambers, is having them to start with.

In Pennsylvania in 2016, Governor Tom Wolf signed a nondiscrimination bill that said that by executive order, people can not discriminate based on race, age, gender, or sexual orientation. Now let's look at how a military person motivates recruits.

Now by the discrimination law we can not as a continuum allow some of the language used to train. "What are you real men?" won't work as this is a form of homophobia. "What are you babies" this neither is allowed under our agreement that is binding all throughout Pennsylvania particularly but all United Nations member states, as this is discrimination based on age. "What are you a bunch of" becomes a dead way to train.

This is the time when we really can say for confirmation that the meek will inherit the earth. In the same way Victor Hugo said, "An idea can outdo any army." When a leader "earns" respect because the same hand that feeds you, also went and hid the food... this isn't really a real form of respect but transference, and is not in keeping with a "progressive" ideal of leadership. The same with many public positions, if people only like you because of your blackmail ability, it is not true respect. When you have true love for yourself you can begin with the right tools to really see over the houses that are built on the sand. And the confederacy can die very quickly, in all our countries.

Inhumane is anything that would strip a person of their cloak of humanity. When you have a part of Civil Rights or Human Rights that is taken away from a person, it follows that it is discriminatory and is very inhumane. Humanity is something that can not be stripped away. Your humanity is what gives you equality with all others. If something begins to present an inequality, by discrimination of human rights, that becomes out of alignment, and a violation of the United

Nations charter. If you have to ask, is this inhumane, then you should know that it is.

Degrading has to do with the inequality, of singling out a person based on their race or sexuality, or other Civil Rights category. The degrading is how you know, if it is meant to help or to hinder, which is against all human rights.

Article 6

Everyone has the right to recognition everywhere as a person before the law.

Everybody please read Article 6 for yourself. Then you can read my interpretation. All the document helps interpret itself, by all the articles working together to promote a message and a tone of what human rights looks like. This article is about the concept of recognition. It states that everyone has the right to recognition everywhere as a person before the law. This is very important today because anybody who is under 18 has no recognition in a subservient law, to either positive or negative rights. The document even adds that their recognition is as a person before the law.

Personhood begins to have recognition at conception and it continues from age 1 to 100+, until it trails in their departing. Now let's approach recognition from the idea of liberty. A person has the right to recognition, and to be "as a person" under the law. This is overreached in many forms of servitude by power of attorney, and the government at large in many aspect, and to subservient collective agreements. That a person of a young age is under necessity of a guardian, it could be said that a parent has permission, or that right of guardianship over the recognition of an individual. This gives parents permission over the recognition rights of their young, but does not fully cancel the young from their equality of voice that they have a right to just by being part of the human membership.

The virtue is that everyone under 18 in the United States, or any manifestation of under age, in dealing with government representation, age of consent, age of voting, age of drinking, age of driving, in all its manifestations is not to ever take away the right of recognition especial in the young and personhood in their liberty and equality of voice. In any decision that the young person wants to make, there should be an age of chivalrous consent, where they can have all the rights granted by agreement to all peoples. It is not for others to use the law, to speak for them. None of the agreements that determine by age, are in alignment with the UN charter and especially Article 6. The rights of consent of people under 18 in the United States is a very big Civil Rights issue.

When this overreaches transgressions against an individual, and become in Romeo and Juliet cases, about the separation of star-crossed lovers just because it is a law, it is a very bad, ill informed, way of using the lawagreement which is suppose to align with nature. It is also out of alignment with the higher virtues of Human Rights. So a human has the same rights across the board without distinction from age pre-birth to transition. In the case of the very real situation that a guardian would have to hold these rights for another, it should be only to guide that voice not in the image of the guardian, but in the expression of permission. If we will use the Age of Consent in America and say one is 17, and the other is 18, the 17 year old can ask permission for courtship allowances to the mother and father, and if the mother and father say no, then it is a case of permission of transgression, or permission of consent, that is a secondary violation if the 18 year old transgresses even under consent of the 17 year old. If the parents say yes to the relationship, then the laws of consent are fulfilled. Parents hold permission as the one necessity over the recognition of the young. The recognition however is highlighted in this document as reigning supreme over the liberty transgressed by the permission.

So to ask about what the correct age of consent is, transgresses the right of recognition and right of persons. The correct way to go about it is to acknowledge that the young has liberty, and that liberty in the growing process is under permission of the parents. In any situation of equals before the law, transgression is the violation of the liberty of another. In the case of minor law, it is very discriminatory to put the young without equality. In the case of minor law, moving to the higher octave of permission consent, it makes consent then something that is between not just a person and another, but a person, a permission, and another. So therefore the voices of the guardians are the farthest reach that the agreement can stretch. Remember, right to liberty and life and security of persons, in the spirit of brotherhood is what we aim for in human rights. Your true love is not to be taken away because of the law agreement, that is not what agreements are made to do.

Article 7

All are equal before the law and are entitled without discrimination to equal protection of the law. All are entitled to equal protection against any discrimination in violation of this Declaration and against any incitement to such discrimination.

Now we have arrived at article 7. Please read it and study and ponder it for yourself. This commandment ushers in a new concept called "incitement." Now one of my favorite documents of reference is the 2015 bill that bans conversion therapy for sexual orientation under Barack Obama called HR 2450. I like to call this the Anoka Hennepin Act, as this was the school district that had many children take their life because of the harsh attitude towards people being gay, or lesbian, or transgender or allies.

This conversion idea is an incitement to discrimination. Often times ignorance is overlooked for religious concepts. I myself was always on the fence not knowing what God's will would be on the subject. He endowed me with great questions and the God seeking heart of David, to seek solutions on this. And I pray that you will accept like I did that sexual orientation is not life or death. In 2012 watching the Republican debates and seeking into this I really wanted to know the correct religious position. Jesus mentions that in regard to marriage in Matthew 19, "some will be born eunuchs from their mother's womb." Now in the Western World I grew up in, the concept of eunuch meant chaste. But in the anthropology and paradigm of the time the Bible was written the correct interpretation for eunuch is "third gendered." A concept of the eunuch today would be what we call gay, lesbian, and transgender. Jesus was speaking about this topic when he spoke about marriage.

Now with the writings of Paul, to accept his teachings as laws is not good theology. The 3 major religions in the world spring from the Biblical Adam. Moses gives us the Torah which are the 613 commandments. The Torah is the first 5 books of the Bible. Starting with the book of Joshua through the last book of the Old Testament Malachi there is no new laws. Now when Jesus comes to bring the new covenant many Jews like Paul are harshly resistant to his one command, "love as I have loved." It is a huge leap to move from the Jewish Torah of Moses to the teachings of Christ, the Anointed of God. Now when Paul comes and gives new commands, these are now separate from the laws given to Moses, and the fulfillment through Jesus Christ. To read the Pauline books as many do, like the Torah or the Gospels is incorrect.

Jesus also had the beloved disciple, whom I advocate the research into and I endorse the teachings of the Berean Church. This relationship between Jesus and the Beloved Disciple, was inter generational much like the inter generational relationships of all the gods of the Greeks and Romans. There is a document called "The Secret Gospel of Mark" that would allude that such a relationship was best said, "special" and really brings the Gospels new clarity to know the author of the Gospel of John.

The beautiful document HR 2450 says, "being lesbian, gay, bisexual, transgender or gender nonconforming is not a disorder, disease, or illness, deficiency or shortcoming;

The national community of professionals in education, social work, health, mental health, and counseling has determined that there is no scientifically valid evidence for attempting to prevent a person from being lesbian, gay, bisexual, transgender, or gender nonconforming."

Anything as such that targets a part of the essential self is something that qualifies as an incitement to discrimination. And all manifestations of the incitement in many categories such as neurodiversity such as ADHD or Autism, is what the UN Declaration considers you free from with protection on up to the highest agreement, any incitement to discrimination, with non-distinction.

Article 8

Everyone has the right to an effective remedy by the competent national tribunals for acts violating the fundamental rights granted him by the constitution of by law.

Please read over article number 8, and meditate and study on it. We are given through this commandment the idea of "effective remedy." During the presidential cycle in 2016 I was talking to a friend about Jill Stein and I learned a new word that she campaigned on. The new word that I learned was called "reparations." Jill Stein believes that we owe civil rights and specifically the African American community reparations for what we had put them through. I asked my friend what does a reparation look like, and he said, "I'm not sure if anybody knows what reparations look like, but they are necessary." And I got a glimpse of what the moving paradigm looks like and this aligns with the concept of effective remedy. Jill Stein is right, we need to move from the mindset of suing that is looking for gain, to the concept of seeking reparations, which is looking for equality.

The concept of effective remedy is a term of completion. There is not meant to be open ended disputes in lawagreement. The way effective remedy works is that there should be in all cases, reparations in full. That is to say that the justice system was not meant to be a marketplace. Anybody who is going through edification by the tribunals should be in the system long enough to repair relationships. Effective Remedy means a sense of completion and graduation, for all humans to be made healthy, maintaining equality and non-distinction. All finances should be equally returned to all humans, with life, liberty and security in exact reparation.

Article 9

No one shall be subjected to arbitrary arrest, detention, or exile.

Read article 9 and meditate upon it. There is something interesting here and that is the use that this document uses in certain commands of the word "arbitrary." Now following the collective agreement this does mean that arrest is something that is allowed under the United Nations, and the security and safety of people is the reason for that. If we have the right to reason we can look at the world at large and see that there are some things, that are ideas, "principalities and powers" that are not beneficial. This is where we have to discern. The use of the word arbitrary makes us open for interpretation as if there was not a command at all. I will say that the values of this document serve to limit the powers of the (unnatural) system. And this document serves to articulate human dignity and value. And this document serves to give the individual effective remedy.

This is a very big topic. I would like to list some of the people from history who have been arrested; Jesus Christ, John the Baptist, Peter, Paul, Silas, Joseph, Martin Luther King Jr., Nelson Mandela, William Penn. I wish I could give reparations to Nelson Mandela for what life we took away from him. We can give reparations to him by stop crucifying people, for any reason. When we think of Jesus, we think that he overcame the grave. But we also have to reason that we put him up, the man who carried all the sins of the world, to the worst of human experiences on the cross. Think of the sinlessness of Jesus Christ, the Lamb of God, when thinking about this subject, and maybe we can articulate a better world for our posterity.

This introduces a new concept that I want to call the *pyranade*. I call it pyranade because of the shiny color of the pyrite rocks. All people are born of the light, and often times they hold views that are counter to the established system. Think of Rosa Parks taking that seat on the bus and what it did for human rights future. So the people who are of the system profit off of the pyranade, and the system is judgmental. A person who follows Jesus command "lest ye judge, you will be judged" will be called like Dr. King in his crusade of "nonviolent resistance" to lower themselves in their thoughts to interact with the system. This person is not of the system, but now resonant with it, and they lose a little bit of their shine. I acknowledge that glow that every human has the right to, by calling all people in the Christ-Help-Us Justice System, pyrandes. So a person is arrested and is then put through the system for the purpose of this writing until the time of their effective remedy, is called a pyranade.

Effective Remedy itself is a form of civil rights. Articles 9, 10, 11 all deal with pyranade agreement. It is a major crux of our human experience that needs some new love and new ideas. This is to say everyone in captivity as a pyranade we need to find some sanity in our values. Jacque Fresco of The Venus Project was a very wise mentor of mine, and he taught that society will change when our hearts and values do.

This document is the nexus of our human agreement. This is where the idea of captivity of the human begins. It begins with the **integrity for limitation** by use of the word "**arbitrary**" and therefore we want to recognize within the pyranade the fruit and the virtue of the whole document.

Article 10

Everyone is entitled in full equality to a fair and public hearing by an independent and impartial tribunal, in the determination of his rights and obligations of any criminal charges against him.

Please read over article 10 and meditate on it. This is the first articulation in the agreement about the concept of obligations. Now obligations are preceded by rights. The rights are the ones spelled out in this document. It is the 10th article of the United Nations Declaration of Human Rights. What do we know of the values so far is that the pyranade has life, liberty, and security of person with non-distinction and through any case has access to effective remedy. Now at this time it would be of benefit to read Section 3 of this book entitled "Courting."

Your rights will empower your virtue, and we all seek out same and similar virtues. The idea of a court system is to settle disputes. That should be its only goal is restitution and equilibrium. Since there is no arbitrary arrests then it would be very few humans who would be outside of their rights where they would have to go before a court in a negative sense. The court should in every case be there as a positive institution towards creating agreements.

To get two to become one in Christ is a very wise virtue. It is the privilege of the forgiven to forgive. Any finance standing in the way of that is contrary to the values of the United Nation Declaration. And so I hope to see a revival of the courts with new faces, new virtues, and these 30 commandments should be paramount to anything that takes place within them.

Obligations are something that people will have if they are found in transgression of restitution and a path should be laid for the redemption of the pyranade and the restoration of relationships. In keeping in mind that the pyranade, like all humans under this declaration, have a right to effective remedy, and reparations in full, at the end of their case. So now nobody benefits from the transgression or sin but benefits from reconciling.

Our justice system was built on the backs of slaves, and therefore the judicial system has never been adequate to represent equality. I purpose calling the three branches of government the legislative, the executive, and the reparations branch. For our posterity we want the agreement to surround ethics and morals, and not financial motivation.

Article 11

> Everyone charged with a penal offence has the right to be presumed innocent until proved guilty according to the law in a public trial at which he has had all guarantees necessary for his defence.

> No one shall be held guilty of any penal offence on account of any act or omission which did not constitute a penal offence, under national or international law, at the time when it was committed. Nor shall a heavier penalty be imposed than the one that was applicable at the time the penal offence was committed.

Please read over article 11, and mediate and pray about it. This article will be strengthened by the clarity of further articles to come. This discerns the differences between a person who is innocent and otherwise. I believe Christ to be guiltless, and my faith is in his propitiation blood. Part of the agreement is social and what your peers say. You are to be given "all guarantees necessary for defense." This is after hearing your rights. As an innocent person you maintain all rights, so before court in the segment of coming to an agreement, you have all the rights of any other human with non-distinction. And you maintain your human rights at the outset of the edification by the court. Court is meant to be a very small part of life.

Now I want to introduce a new word and the new word is the andronade. Andromeda in mythology was the chained women, who was waiting for someone to come and save her. In Christ is our salvation, but we also acknowledge that faith without works is dead. If someone goes into these topics that are humanitarian, they are andronades who are to support the pyranades. This is for all of those who want to give a cup of cold water to even the least of these.

Jesus had a descending nature rather than one of ascent in his Earthly walk. That is while most of humanity looks to elevate themselves, he saw the virtue in going to the back of the line. I call this "deep sea fishers of men." That nature in a human being is a rarity but it is one of extreme bravery. The andronades are the ones who want to free all humanity, and recognize that the interest of one is not separate from the whole.

The conversation of this topic should be about stability of the andronades in extending their love to people who are pyranades on up to being on death row. Jesus did not accept the testimony of man, because he knew what was in them. We want to look upon all people through the blood of the lamb and our own equality.

To call you not innocent is something that man will do. I see this concept like chicken pox, it seems you don't want to talk about it but everyone seems to get them once in their life. James in the Bible, said "count it all joy when you are going through trials of many kinds." And it should be left to personal responsibility to influence the world in the direction that your life experience has called you to pray for.

Article 12

No one shall be subjected to arbitrary interference with his privacy, family, home or correspondence, nor to attacks upon his honour and reputation. Everyone has the right to the protection of the law against such interference or attacks.

Please read and pray, and ponder on article 12. There is to be no arbitrary interference in your life. With non-distinction and under the Nation States of the United Nations there is to be no interference allowed in correspondence. Thus people make circuits of which no body can interfere and be a circuit breaker.

So you have the right to correspond with who you want to correspond with. If somebody does not like your company, they have the virtue of influence but they can not direct your path. You only need ask a person, "How would you like somebody interfering in your correspondence, on your honour, on your reputation?" and they will respond with empathy.

On your honour and reputation nobody can attack that. This includes non-distinction of all categories under the moniker "human" and also civil rights such as race, gender identity, sexuality, and gender expression.

Article 13

> ➤ Everyone has the right to freedom of movement and residence within the borders of each State.
> ➤ Everyone has the right to leave any country, including his own, and to return to his country

Please read article 13 and mediate and ponder over it's meaning. Everybody has freedom of movement. What are the implications of this? Everyone has the freedom to move within the states and countries under the UN. This means there is nothing stopping or preventing people from crossing the borders.

This is also true of people who want to leave the country. The people have the right to leave a country and also to reenter. There is no financial advantage to transfers of states and countries, with non-distinction. Everyone has the freedom to "disperse" across state and country lines. All throughout the 193 Nation States any one under the moniker of human is free to roam, per the UN charter, to all 193 countries.

Article

14

> Everyone has the right to seek and to enjoy in other countries asylum from persecution.

> This right may not be invoked in the case of prosecutions genuinely arising from non-political crimes or from acts contrary to the purposes and principles of the United Nations.

Read over the article and articulate it for yourself. This has to do with the concept of freedom of asylum. To all the nation states under the UN – any one looking to flee the country they live in for political, civil rights issues, all countries under the UN agreed to let all people in.

This conversation of immigration is our responsibility to welcome all who need asylum. The sanctuary cities are good ideas, in the sense these cities should be designed to speed up the process of citizenship. Possibly within these designated immigration cities there can possibly be a temporary asylum license that is as equal as citizenship for refugees.

Remember each country may need to organize their system of immigration. Generally you are a part of a larger family, and larger membership of the United Nations where you have the right to enter the 193 countries in equality. UN membership is a permission slip to path to citizenship in any of the Member State countries.

Article 15

- ➢ Everyone has the right to a nationality.
- ➢ No one shall be arbitrarily deprived of his nationality nor denied the right to change nationality.

Please read and mediate upon article 15. This article concerns the topic of the right to nationality. Each system of the nations has its own priorities in ushering people into their country. This however is not the place of nexus to focus on. The issue is not do you accommodate the country, but will they accommodate the individual. I should hope you want to improve the country of which you belong in return. Nationality can not be denied a person. You always have your nationality, on the high plateau of the gestalt values of those who wrote the Declaration following the war. The first clause says in full that everyone has the right to nationality. In a secondary clause it does again mention this word "arbitrary" in relation to nationality. This should be something to be seen as very limited and of ethnocentric cultural concern.

The paradigm is that you have equality of nationality access throughout the 193 Nation states. This land is available with all benefits of citizenship to all people, with the liberty to chose which country best suits them. Rights of the UN agreement, higher then all nation states, should make human rights the nexus of what the country government implements in terms of immigration policies.

Article 16

> Men and women of full age, without any limitation due to race, nationality or religion, have the right to marry and to found a family. They are entitled to equal rights as to marriage, during marriage and at its dissolution.
> Marriage shall be entered into only with the free and full consent of the intending spouses.
> The family is the natural and fundamental group unit of society and is entitled to protection by society and the State.

Please read over this article on a very important topic of equal rights in marriage. This article concerns the rights of couples to consent to marry each other and individuals to marry who they want. Marriage should be of full consent between the two people. Marriage is given precedence over society and family is a protected institution under the agreement.

The stipulations are that "men and women" "of full age" are allowed to marry without limitation. The idea of "without limitation" is beautiful knowing that ideas and mores concerning marriage, as they have throughout history and culture, have evolved since 1948. The UN document is to promote per the preamble, "social progress" in keeping up with the newer expressions of marriage. It remains that two very important distinctions are made. People have the right to consent, and people have the right to say no.

Ron Paul is a modern day politician who I personally find reputable. He was asked in his dedication to libertarian principles, "what are your views on marriage." He said that people should be allowed to do what they want and call it what they want. Such a statement matches the integrity of the American experiment and also the very freedom afforded by the intentions of the signers of The United Nations Declaration of Human Rights.

Article 17

> ➢ Everyone has the right to own property alone as well as in association with others.
> ➢ No one shall be arbitrarily deprived of his property.

Please study article 17 for yourself, and meditate upon it. This article is about the right to property. In the US all 30 of our amendments are covered in great ways by the United Nations declaration. For example, "right to bare arms" in the US is spelled out more generally as the right to own property.

This is to say that you have a right, a human right, to your belonging and valuables. No one shall be arbitrarily deprived of property. This is to say all rightful things belonging to you are your property. You can own property by yourself or in association with others.

In article 22 it is revealed that all have access to social security. This is to say you have the right to your own property. There is yet the clause of arbitrary in this command to leave it open ended. But the affirmative is overwhelmingly to let people have property. Our world has decided under the UN in 1948 that property is King over all arguments of prohibition and this includes the concept of gun control because that is a form of property. This is to fit that man is seen as basically good and given equal responsibility with all citizens.

Article 18

Everyone has the right to freedom of thought, conscience and religion; this right includes freedom to change his religion or belief, and freedom, either alone or in community with others and in public or private, to manifest his religion or belief in teaching, practice, worship, and observance.

Please I encourage the reader to study and mediate on this article 18. This article is about having the freedom of thought, and conscience and religion. These human rights extend from the idea of liberty, which is expansive. Your freedom of conscience is a very valuable thing and there are big implications in the fullest realization of this document. You are allowed to worship and to teach any way that speaks to your conscience.

You have the freedom to think in alignment with your conscience. Some names like Nicholas Copernicus, and Charles Darwin faced criticism of heresy for their ideas of conscience. Copernicus was called a heretic for his view of the Sun centered Solar System, until his works were confirmed to be accurate. Darwin tried to match his conscience of what he knew to be true from his natural studies to the faith that he learned in his local church. He would walk around in the night with the burden of conscience.

Any form of worship is an extension of the fruits of a person's conscience. These ideas may not always agree with yours, but they are genuine to a person's life experience. There is no clause to say that people are not given right to their own conscience.

Article 19

Everyone has the right to freedom of opinion and expression; this right includes freedom to hold opinions without interference and to seek, receive and impart information and ideas through any media and regardless of frontiers.

Please read over article 19 and mediate on it. Article 19 builds on article 18. I can envision that someone questioned at the original meeting the freedom of thought, and someone else said, "well you also have the freedom of opinion." This article is very close to the first amendment which is often called freedom of expression. This also can be called "freedom of media." The freedom of media is that everyone has the right to express your thoughts and opinions, regardless of frontiers. Nobody can interfere with your relationship to seek, receive and impart information.

Article 19 gives you access to freedom of your own thoughts, including freedom of expression. Now this right to freedom is to both media and the principle extends to today's technology. You are allowed to spread your ideas, impart information and ideas through any media regardless of frontiers. You know that Jesus was the most controversial figure of all times, and we have this freedom to be opinionated and even controversial. We have this freedom to impart genuine thoughts which is not to be a question.

Article 20

> Everyone has the right to freedom of peaceful assembly and association.
> No one may be compelled to belong to an association

Please read this important article 20. One of my favorite politicians is Ron Paul. He would often on principle vote no on spending bills often alone to the over 400 who voted yes. This is something that I see as a big virtue. One person who protests is as valuable to the system as any other part of it. Sometimes standing alone is the right thing to do.

Everyone under the UN has the right to do citizen audits. That is in all manners people can gather in peaceful assembly to protest and petition. Just as beautiful as any group, is the one who can stand alone in what he believes in. This is why protesting and peaceful assembly is a good thing and healthy thing that people have access to alone, or in association.

Protest cannot interfere with the rights of property. All public places are subject to the citizens, and all government offices are subject to people audits. This is because the public work serves the private work, so the citizen is the boss of the representative. This virtue of peaceful assembly should be a mutual relationship the government representative and the citizen share.

I would suggest reading the writings of Martin Luther King Jr in "A Testament of Hope" and his understanding of the role and scope that the peaceful assembly plays in the movement of civil rights. It is truly a remarkable read.

Article 21

> Everyone has the right to take part in the government of his country, directly or through freely chosen representatives.
> Everyone has the right to equal access to public service in his country.
> The will of the people shall be the basis of the authority of government; this will shall be expressed in periodic and genuine elections which shall be by universal and equal suffrage and shall be held by secret vote or by equivalent free voting procedures.

Please read over article 21. What article 21 talks about is that everyone in their country has the right to take part in government either directly or through the voting process. This is an important plateau of "resting ascension" that any one has the right and equal access to run for any position in the government.

The article does not stipulate that there is to be certain times or processes for elections, just that there be "periodic" expressions of the will of the people within the country. All elections are within the bounds of the nexus of this UN document, and these 30 commandments as parameters.

This means that per the UN Declaration all pyranades are allowed to vote in their country, and they are also allowed to run and be seated if they receive the votes of the people. William Penn was a pyranade for his philadelphian views in England. He came over here with those same beliefs that were not accepted in his home country, and created his Philadelphia for religious freedom in the new world as the state of Pennsylvania. Joseph of Genesis was a pyranade in Egypt the land of his captivity, but he followed the will of God and became Pharaoh of Egypt.

Our votes are very important as they give access to the whole of abundance through equality of influence in raising revenue. Our votes represent our liberty, represent our conscience, and represent our expression.

Article 22

Everyone, as a member of society, has the right to social security and is entitled to realization, through national effort and international co-operation and in accordance with the organization and resources of each State, of the economic, social and cultural rights indispensable for his dignity and the free development of his personality.

Please read this very important article 22, and mediate and pray about it and ponder what it looks like in the fullest realization of human rights. This one states that everyone has the right to social security. Now what does that mean? Remember Eleanor Roosevelt's husband Franklin D Roosevelt created the structure for social security. The meaning of what Eleanor had in mind spearheaded this in articulation of what social security is, would mean something close to a social security check. Now I would propose calling this an "appreciation wage" for each person who needs access to resources that will bring to them social security in the free and full development of his personality.

The language of United Nations Declaration of Human Rights gives ear to all persons for social security. This right or grace is to mean every person. This compliance should look towards the least among within the local jurisdiction, this includes ESPECIALLY those in situations of obligation including those who are pyranades even in captivity and those in the military.

Part of reading a persons rights include social security, their subservience to an "Appreciation Wage" or an allowance for being first eternal and secondary human. All those currently detained as pyranades shall be granted accrual of Social Security, through a new Financial Management program with the finance of the "Appreciation Wage" coming from the local jurisdiction to begin a process to get people to see all humans as equal.

All persons under obligation should be accruing in compounding interest, money for them through the standard Appreciation Wage or Social Security each month as they have the right to, and equally entitled to be made aware of. Each person in the justice system, civil system, or military should be getting to know their rights to Social Security, and they are entitled to realization.

Article 23

- Everyone has the right to work, to free choice of employment, to just and favourable conditions of work and to protection against unemployment.
- Everyone, without any discrimination, has the right to equal pay for equal work.
- Everyone who works has the right to just and favourable remuneration ensuring for himself and his family an existence worthy of human dignity, and supplemented, if necessary, by other means of social protection.
- Everyone has the right to form and to join trade unions for the protection of his interests.

Please read over article 23 and pray about it and mediate on it. This one concerns the idea of the right to work. Now everyone has the free choice to seek out a place to work and to earn a living through that. Anybody without discrimination should receive equal pay for equal work. This is the side of the understanding of employment. And the work environment should have favorable conditions.

At the same time while at the place of work everyone has the right to form and to unionize. And also when not working the declaration gives ear to receiving compensation for unemployment as well.

Article 24

Everyone has the right to rest and leisure, including reasonable limitation of working hours and periodic holidays with pay.

Please read article 24 and understand and mediate upon it. This pertains to the idea of the right to work. While you are at your place of work you also have benefits of working. These include vacation time where you can rest from the work that you do. You are also given such benefits as holiday pay for the work that you do.

Article 25

- Everyone has the right to a standard of living adequate for the health and well-being of himself and of his family, including food, clothing, housing, and medical care and necessary social services, and the right to security in the event of unemployment, sickness, disability, widowhood, old age or other lack of livelihood in circumstances beyond his control.
- Motherhood and childhood are entitled to special care and assistance. All children, whether born in or out of wedlock, shall enjoy the same social protection.

Please read article 25 and mediate on it, and pray about it. Now this UN25 is one of great humanitarian aids in the tool belt of the individual looking to make a change. Abraham Maslow created the theory of Hierarchy of Needs. That is all humans need food, water, shelter and love. And from the meeting of a persons basic needs they can begin to actualize their personality, which is a goal of the Declaration.

The United Nations Declaration lists as a human right for all, adequate living for the health of each person, and well-being of each person. This includes especially in situations of the least among in the conditions of both pyranades, and military (and all similar) training.

To spell out the fullest actualization of this system there should be an interactive measure, to make sure that each person under any jurisdiction is able to voice adequate health, and adequate well-being concerns. This is how important human rights compliance is, and this UN document has all constitutions of Member States in subservience. There should be two end user documents for "Health Audit" and "Well-Being Audit" and these concerns should go before local jurisdiction in order to sort, as well as written in a public registry where there can be a 3rd "Family Audit" where family members can petition on record for finding human rights alignment.

Not everybody has the same values, so inevitably this is never going to be a perfect system but it is in alignment with moving the needle towards human rights. The greatest shall serve the least, on up to and especially last.

I purpose under 25UN putting a spotlight on foundations. In places of detainment or non consent these are the most important UN audits, that each person has rights to adequate food, clothing, water, and shelter, and more. There should be the ability for people to make sure that all those under a jurisdiction starting with the foundations, which include those places of little oversight, like the military and the justice system, and the prisons receive adequate human rights satisfaction.

What are the foundations? These are the places that are often overlooked, given their own cloak of darkness where corruption of human rights can be a normative. These places are recognized to be secondary to human rights, and the higher octave awareness does have a handle on the inevitability of people gravitating to positions where they can be an authority without subservience. These are the place where human rights shall shine the spotlight on higher virtue.

Starting with the identification of the foundations, people can personally audit under the UN compliance to the public and representatives of the jurisdiction. All City Compliance should first start with all geographical foundations within the jurisdiction, including federal places to be compliant to state and local property. In addition, there should be spotlights, whom will inspect these places to bring higher virtue into the standing systems, to find alignment with UN and human rights compliance.

I have much more on this topic of article 25 in Section 5
of this book called "City Accompaniment."

Article 26

- ➢ Everyone has the right to education. Education shall be free, at least in the elementary and fundamental stages. Elementary education shall be compulsory. Technical and professional education shall be made generally available and higher education shall be equally accessible to all on the basis of merit.
- ➢ Education shall be directed to the full development of the human personality and to the strengthening of respect for human rights and fundamental freedoms. It shall further the activities of the United Nations for the maintenance of peace.
- ➢ Parents have a prior right to choose the kind of education that shall be given to their children

Please read article 26 and pray and mediate upon it. This article concerns the freedom of education. Education for the elementary and fundamental stages should be free. And then when you move on to higher education it is then on the basis of merit. Parents are allowed to chose the education that their children can receive.

Article 27

> Everyone has the right freely to participate in the cultural life of the community, to enjoy the arts and to share in scientific advancement and its benefits.
> Everyone has the right to the protection of the moral and material interests resulting from any scientific, literary or artistic production of which he is the author.

Please read article 27 and meditate upon it. Everyone is entitled to promote the human rights and achieve their fullest manifestation of personality through the community. Everyone should be involved in the community to participate in the cultural life and share in the movement of technology and science.

Everyone is allowed to participate in community events and the cultural life of the community. This is an article about expression in relation to the sharing of the community and all it's benefits. Now this article also talks about the idea of intellectual property that is a very big one. The article says that an artist has a right to his art. That is the moral and material interests resulting from any production is given protection through the UN Declaration. This means that the artist has access to his songs, has access to his media, has access to his photos, has access to his writings and is in control of his intellectual property in the promotion of moral and material interests of which he or she is the author.

Article 28

Everyone is entitled to a social and international order in which the rights and freedoms set forth in this Declaration can be fully realized.

Please read article 28 and ponder over it, and meditate on it. This article is about an order that each person has on up to international resources for the maintaining of their Human Rights. This would be through the court system that is mentioned in UN10 to allot rights and obligations. Courting as in Section 3 is about the atonement of relationships and the restitution of the counter balance. A pyranade goes through the edification experience knowing that he has the right to effective remedy, which is reparations in full.

This means that every court under the United Nations charter is to positively promote these 30 commandments. And if you know of the gestalt need for human rights, then there is never any worries but always solutions. For this to be fully realized we need to learn about the blueprint of the court system and start to follow virtues. If you turn on American television there are a lot of shows that show we have let go of sanity in relationship to what virtue is.

I used to enjoy watching Dateline with my grandma and eating a bologna sandwich. I miss her very much as she has since passed on. Today I embrace the vegetarian paradigm because I don't see an animal as bologna. For the same reason I care about animal rights, I don't watch shows where you drone to "who done it" for no purpose other than entertainment. Jesus said your body is a temple, and when you truly realize what you are feeding your eyes and what you are feeding your soul, you can never go back and you have to move forward as I talk about in Section 3 on Courting.

Article 29

> Everyone has duties to the community in which alone the free and full development of his personality is possible.
> In the exercise of his rights and freedoms, everyone shall be subject only to such limitations as are determined by law solely for the purpose of securing due recognition and respect for the rights and freedoms of others and of meeting the just requirements of morality, public order, and the general welfare in a democratic society.
> These rights and freedoms may in no case be exercised contrary to the purposes and principles of the United Nations.

Please meditate on article 29, and ponder it for yourself. This has to do with the free and full development of the human personality. Now this means that you have the singular responsibility to promote this Declaration in all areas. By UN29 it is your duty to the community to make sure that these rights are maintained and looked after, as the nexus of all subservient agreements.

I purpose that people start to form "Compliance Alliances" in their town or city. The "Compliance Alliance" should look out for these rights being maintained as a central aspect of the community, involved in all community projects. I purpose that they assume that it is a top down project to get each local jurisdiction into compliance, changing everything to conform with the blueprint of the 30 golden commandments. Chances are that there is rampant disregard for human rights and there will be people who cling to the old wine. As someone Compliant you are purposing the new glass of the future. This Declaration of Human Rights is an elevated document that involves a higher order of thinking and feeling. You have access to and through this document to peaceful assembly, and this is a very positive cause to organize and assemble around.

I purpose that you learn the whole structure of your city in relationship to Human Rights through the section 5 in this book "City Accompaniment", and that there be a time every year of 30 weeks, where each week one of the Human Rights is promoted and explored and given open forum in a community audit of all foundations where the least among us is.

Article 30

Nothing in this Declaration may be interpreted as implying for any State, group, or person any right to engage in any activity or to perform any act aimed at the destruction of any of the rights and freedoms set forth herein.

Read article 30 and mediate upon it. This is the empowerment of the document to say that the Declaration is a complete works to interpret itself as a unit, rather than the sum of its parts. This is not to be confused with the Commandments of the Bible, these 30 golden commandments serve as a nexus towards law agreement and the evolution of social progress throughout all the land. They are written by mortal human hands, who sought the virtue of a better world of peace and tranquility.

This UN Book can now serve as the completion, for all 193 Nation States, of the conversation about Human Rights in the world, in all of federal, state, and local jurisdictions. So not only do you have the Andrew interpretations to start the conversation, but in the back of the book is a full copy of the Declaration, and there is a customization for you to jot down your own notes on each of the 30 commandments in interaction with the world that you live in.

With UN 29, I purpose the foot soldiers of the "Compliance Alliance" form to express their duty to the community in seeing that all our communities have the fullest realization of human rights. I purpose that we think of our work with "Compliance Alliance" as a tithe, of 1/10 of a person's time. I don't want people to lose their life, family, and friends over the deep sea fishing. But we can see the agape, unconditional gestalt love, for all of humanity as part of this relationship to the community and it is a special call and not meant for everybody. There is a lot of content here to become educated on this topic, to start conversations about the topic, and create a better world for the pyranade and all the andronades, for posterity, and for the full development of the human personality.

UN BOOK

Section 2

Jesus Teachings

Here are some of Jesus teachings and principles that I will share with you in an order that I have found helpful in the process of the prayers that inspired the UN Book.

Love Your Enemy

Matthew 6:43

"You have heard that it was said, 'Love your neighbor. Hate your enemy.' But here is what I tell you. Love your enemies. Pray for those who hurt you. Then you will be sons of your Father who is in Heaven."

70 x 7

Matthew 18:21-22

"Then came Peter to him, and said, Lord, how oft shall my brother sin against me, and I forgive him? Till seven times? Jesus saith unto him, "I say not unto thee, until seven times, until seventy times seven."

Judge Not

Matthew 7:1-2

"Do not judge others. Then you will not be judged. You will be judged in the same way you judge others. You will be measured in the same way you measure others."

99 Sheep

Matthew 18:12-13

"If a man have 100 sheep, and one of them be gone astray, doth he not leave the 99 and goeth into the mountains, and seeketh that which is gone astray? And if so be that he find it, verily I say unto you, he rejoiceth more of that sheep, than the 99 which went astray."

Come For Sinners

Matthew 9:12-13

"They that be whole need not a physician, but they that are sick. But go ye and learn what that meanth, I will have mercy, and not sacrifice for I am not come to call the righteous, but sinners to repentance."

Not Kill

Matthew 5:21-22

"You have heard that it was said by them of old time, thou shall not kill: and whosoever shall kill shall be in danger of judgment: But I say to you that everyone who is angry with his brother will be liable to judgment; and whosoever shall say to his brother, Raca, shall be in danger of the council: but whosoever shall say, thou fool, shall be in danger of hell fire."

Turn the Cheek

Matthew 5:38-39

"You have heard that it hath been said, an eye for an eye, and a tooth for a tooth: But I say unto you, that ye resist not evil: but whosoever shall smite thee on the right cheek, turn to him the other also."

Reconcile to thy Brother

Matthew 5:23-24

"Therefore if thou bring thy gift to the altar, and there rememberest that thy brother hath ought against thee; leave there thy gift before the altar, and go thy way; first be reconciled to thy brother, and then come and offer thy gift."

Take up your Cross

Matthew 16:24

"If any man will come after me, let him deny himself, and take up his cross and follow me."

Seek Ye First

Matthew 6:33

"Seek ye first the Kingdom of God,
and his righteousness; and all these
things shall be added unto you."

Pray for Workers

Matthew 9:37-38

"The harvest truly is plenteous, but the laborers
are few; pray ye therefore the Lord of the harvest,
that he will send forth laborers into his harvest."

Ask and It is Given

Matthew 7:7-9

"Ask, and it shall be given you; seek,
and ye shall find; knock, and it shall be
opened unto you: For everyone that asketh
receiveth; and he that seeketh findeth; and
to him that knocketh it shall be opened."

First Shall Be Last

Matthew 19:30

"Many that are first shall be last,
and the last shall be first."

Go Extra Mile

Matthew 5:41

"And whosoever shall compel thee to
go a mile, go with him twain."

Give To Whom Asks

Matthew 5:42

"Give to him that asketh thee, and from him
that would borrow of thee turn not thou away."

Blessed Are the Peacemakers

Matthew 5:9

"Blessed are the peacemakers: for they
shall be called the children of God."

God or Money

Matthew 6:24

"No man can serve two masters: for either he will hate the one, and love the other; or else he will hold to the one, and despise the other. Ye cannot serve God and money."

My Yoke is Easy

Matthew 11:28-30

"Come unto me, all ye that labor and are heavy
laden, and I will give you rest. Take my yoke upon
you, and learn of me; for I am meek and lowly
in heart; and ye shall find rest unto your souls.
For my yoke is easy, and my burden is light."

Bridegroom is with Them

Matthew 9:15

"Can the children of the bride chamber
mourn, as long as the bridegroom come,
when the bridegroom shall be taken
from them, and then shall they fast."

Take No Thought

Matthew 6:25

"Therefore I say unto you, take no thought for your life, what ye shall drink; nor yet for your body, what ye shall put on. Is not the life more than meat, and the body more than raiment?"

Cast Out Thy Beam

Matthew 7:5

"First cast out the beam out of thine own eye: and then shalt thou see clearly to cast out the mote out of thy brother's eye."

Let Light Shine

Matthew 5:16

"Let your light so shine before men, and that they may see your good works, and glorify your Father which is in heaven."

Repent

Matthew 4:17

"Repent: for the Kingdom of heaven is at hand."

You Can Forgive

Matthew 9:5-6

"For whether is easier, to say, thy sins be forgiven thee; or to say Arise, and walk? But that ye may know that the Son of Man hath power on earth to forgive sins."

Give Your Cloak

Matthew 5:40

"If any man will sue thee at the law, and take away thy coat, let him have thy cloak also."

∪⋂ BOOK

Section 3

Courting

Court: Remember that "court" is short for courting.

The courtlier such as the judge, are there to form the chivalrous duties of blessing marriages, covenants, partnerships, and all manifestations of valid and accepted mutual acknowledgments and agreements.

Exodus 18: Spiritual Origins

After Moses lead God's people out of their oppression in Egypt, he looked after the disputes of the multitude that sojourned with him in the desert. In Exodus 18:13 Moses father in law Jethro asks Moses, "You are the only judge?" Moses answers, "The people come to me to find out what God wants them to do. Any time they don't agree, they come to me. I decide between them. I tell them about God's rules and laws."

Jethro says, "What you are doing is not good. Choose men of ability from all the people. They must have respect for God. You must be able to trust them. They must not try to get money by cheating others. Appoint them as officials over thousands, hundreds, fifties, and tens. Let them serve the people as judges."

So the courts were designed for Moses as a place of settling disputes. Now Jesus has something to say about this that highlights this conversation between Moses and Jethro, 2,000 years later. He tells his followers on his sermon on the mount, (Matthew 5:23-24) "Suppose you are offering your gift at the altar. And you remember there that your brother has something against you. Leave your gift in front of the altar. First go and make peace with your brother. Then come back and offer your gift."

This is a more evolved way of looking at the court as a place of bringing people into equilibrium. The constellation of Libra is the half way point of the zodiacal story. Libra is said to be the scales of balance, that keep all things in equilibrium. The court is the aiding of Libra in a jurisdiction, and is not meant to be "lower" but central. In the US constitution it spells out that the legislature can promote arts and the community, and this could be projected through utilization of the Courthouse which is the nexus building of any jurisdiction, and the place where Human Rights should be constantly audited. In the future, I would rename this building something that reflects it being the community center.

The courts should be the place of coming into alignment with the legislative agreement. Think about utilizing the court system as a positive mechanism towards falling in love, and getting married, and starting a family.

10 Stages of "Christ-Help-Us Justice System" Reform

1. Agreement

There are 10 sectors that I have identified as places towards guiding momentum in the direction of the promotion of Human Rights. The first is the idea of the legislature. Per the United Nations Declarations under UN21, if you are a member State of the United Nations, you have the Human Right to run for a position in the legislature. You also have the Human Right to vote for who you want, and you have the Human Right to pursue liberty in influencing your opinions in the public arena.

Jesus said that you cannot serve both God and money. And we need to acknowledge that the Christ-Help-Us Justice System is a marketplace. The Christ-Help-Us Justice System profits and fuels itself off of what I call the "Dollar Bible" and it is the list of sins that you are not suppose to do. The whole Christ-Help-Us Justice System is fueled by the book of "do not." Jesus reinterpreted the "do not" as "do" saying "love your neighbor as yourself." By your fruits you will know them, and I don't see any fruit coming from the Christ-Help-Us Justice System. I've heard it said in Law of Attraction teachings that the Universe does not hear the word "no." If you look at something and say "Yes", you attract it. If you look at something and say "No", you attract it. Attraction works through the focus mechanism. That is why I distinguish the idea of the pyranade in the conversation of "lest ye judge", because when it comes to the values of the Christ-Help-Us Justice System "yes" is not wise, nor is "no." The system itself is the problem not the people. When you fight back, you become it. This opens up to exponents of hypocrisy. We really need to align with the laws of the universe in this.

So there is virtue in "first response" and in some cases temporary timeouts, but when you add financial motivation to their usage, you lose the whole virtue as a little leaven, leavens the whole loaf of bread. But if we all decide to close the Dollar Bible, we can open up sanity. You really want all new people in the legislature, and throughout the court system, who realize the true meaning of those positions. I call the system of profiting off of sin, the "*Red Economy*." I want people to evaluate this for yourself with your conscience and reason, and you may come to see like me this whole system as a pejorative.

I purpose an idea I call "*Price Neutral Revenue*." And that is the pyranade is considered price neutral, and his arrest can not be used to fund anything, but rather create a greater liability on the jurisdiction to hold on to. I purpose canceling the Dollar Bible, and making it price neutral and not profitable. In "Price Neutral Revenue", we acknowledge that "all sin is one, and priced at zero."

This is the start of healing and begins a process I call *incentivism*. Incentivism is the process of graduating pyranades. There should be financial incentive to get people into equilibrium. Some people are financially motivated, and if you create the system of incentivism, it will begin to change the way they look at the world. So this idea of incentivism is a new idea, and I acknowledge that we retrain people to follow that the system of corrections, is meant to be a system of healing. There is an art of incentivism, and that involves restitution if need be, reconciliations, and also a system that has a graduation process, or UN8 "Effective Remedy", which would give incentive to weening us off of this system and bringing reparations to the pyranades in the world whose prayers go up in equality to yours. So I encourage the reader to get involved in the agreement!

Two. Education

Ron Paul was once asked a question about morality. He said, "The morality of a nation follows the morality of the people." And this is very important to know that education and it's teachers, follow the same. Right now the quality of educators in regard to the Christ-Help-Us Justice System and the training of first response, is very poor in relation to what it potentially can be. This is why we have to start to train people on virtues that are becoming of the top minds who dedicate time to the subject. Light makes bowling balls of darkness.

Many people go into justice training with a genuine heart to help people. Many find that they have to put up with a lot they disagree with, in order to do that. What we really need to do is a top down audit on what qualifies as virtues. I purpose implementing something called the "*Reindeer System*" and that is to acknowledge the seven reindeer of the system of reparations. They are the topics of which causes most people to become pyranades. The topics are jealousy, sexuality, drugs, finance, neurodiversity, resistance, and cultural diversity. These are the 7 topics that people need to be educated on, and they will need to have a healthy mastery of the concepts. I associate jealousy with dasher, sexuality with dancer, drugs with prancer, finances with vixion, neurodiversity with comet, resistance with cupid, and doner with cultural diversity. To learn about the seven reindeer is the specialized knowledge that a person should learn. I have also color coded what I call "*Rainbow Reparations*" ; red for jealousy, orange for sexuality, yellow for drugs, green for finances, blue for neurodiversity, purple for resistance, and pink for cultural diversity. I purpose education on creating this Reindeer System of training people how to deal with sin in the community, we want to acknowledge a system where all sin is one, and priced at zero. For more on Rainbow Reparations, please see section 4 of this book.

Three. First Response

Now First Response are those on the front line of this system. These should be men and women who are of a higher consciousness. These are the people who should look out for public safety. First Response should be considered a service, and they should be available when someone in the community has a problem. We want to put people of high virtue in the positions of first response, to keep regulated the ones who may not have gestalt values of Human Rights. I purpose sending all First Response to retrain on the reindeer system. I purpose taking a lot of shows off of TV that glorify gain at the expense of another human being. The function of first response is delicate and we need people who are aware of the responsibility that such a position holds.

Fourth. Representation

Adam Conover in his television program, "Adam Ruins Everything" did a special where he ruined the justice system. In this episode the topic is explored about the public defenders given a larger work load, less pay, and greater discrimination than a private law firm. Many people such as LGBTQ and Civil and Human Rights lawyers do their work pro bono, that is free for the cause. I applaud them. This whole sector is an area though that is very greedy for unjust gain. Many books will talk about the broken system and this is one that aims at fixing it.

Many people have gone into lawyer work with humanitarian interest. We again want to keep the humanitarian interest but sink the values of the Red Economy. A genuine lawyer would celebrate such a cause. We do want the people of the courts to be educated in the 7 categories of reparations, and we do want people to start to take back this system for the cause of human rights. Just as Jesus said, "turn the other cheek", an artist can paint with the canvas as it is presented. God can work through people right where they are.

It is possible that we can do away with this step of needing representation all together, and instead give it to leadership in the church of a person's choice. This is just a stage of people, who can positively begin to flow new waves of grace through the system of reparations. We want to make sure that each lawyer is educated and create with the "Compliance Alliance" ratings on the lawyers. The main information should be free. If you take away the Dollar Bible, this whole system of private representation will have to transform and new markets will form in the expanse of higher virtue. Later in Section 4 "Rainbow Reparations" of this book is a section that explains how everyone will be able to keep their job that they currently have, just in a new uniform.

Fifth. Blue Neighborhood

The Blue Neighborhood comes from a CD by Troye Sivan, that basically says, if you are prisoner on the inside, you are one on the outside. Thus this period of being in the closet, is the time that you spend in the Blue Neighborhood. So the Blue Neighborhood refers to a prison and all the people who get paid from it. This is a foundation for all Andronades, because it is where the least among us live. Jesus says, "I have come so that every prison door will be opened." In relation to the Blue Neighborhood there should be a Church that specializes in "last will be first, and first will be last", in acknowledging each pyranade as a child of God.

I purpose that the value systems deserve an update. Those who are struggling in a place of holding, I do hear you and I hope to create the agreement to bring you home. Jesus saves, and we act out his commands. I want to create the Blue Neighborhood as a central theme of a town that is actually seen as a positive place of correcting, that is open, full of helpful people, and in honor of Troye Sivan,, with a swimming pool. We want to get people out of the Blue Neighborhood and value going home over the darker thoughts of homophobia, and racism, and intolerance that paint in their image, and then begin to fill our public system with values of human rights. Jesus said, "My Yoke is Easy", and I want to show people that even on this topic that is so. City Architects should look at the foundations of a city, including military like training, to start to create the Blue Neighborhood in a way that is humane.

*for andronade definition see article 11.

Sixth. Court

The court is a place that should be graced by Human Rights. It is meant to be a place of bringing two together, as in husband and wife. It is a place of reconciliation. The judge should share the virtue of bringing things into equilibrium. If there is money as the virtue in courtlier motivation, then the whole virtue is meaningless. Right now we need to see that the values of the culture, produce individual's of like kind. So that is to say that we need judges, who are aware and virtue reparations and then the job of the judge, will be very easy. When the Blue Neighborhood is a respectable place of healing, the judges could do some of their dealings remotely. This would speed up the process for the pyranade and their families, and also make the courthouse a place that is dealing with positive things, and the measure of a courthouse and a city will be it's work in their understanding of incentivism.

Seventh. Probation

The idea of a probationary period for a person is a sector of the current system. In the future I see it being transformed as a place where there are the 7 categories towards getting people reparations. The people who work in this field shall be trained in the reindeer categories, and they will work with people in the Blue Neighborhood under the category of red. The idea of probation is very close to the concept of prohibition, and these types of ideas of resistance tend to teach that they are not ideal, as prohibition was lifted. I think without the Dollar Bible, we're going to find a lot of these old wines outdated for the fruit of new the ideas under a "price neutral revenue" ready system.

Eighth. Secondaries

At times there will be secondary programs that surround the pyranade experience. These are hopefully going to be incorporated into the main system of reparations for people. To go to a secondary system should be by consent of the person to partake on their own volition. I don't wish any businesses or people to lose their livelihood, but to be transformed and evolved to a system of higher virtue. Such programs can still be there for people who seek out help, just not indirectly financed by the Red Economy. The fruit of these programs can still remain, but done in the condensed form of the Rainbow program. If a person then wishes for a private program by a provider, then that should be financed by the jurisdiction.

Nine. Apartheid

If you are segregated from the group, or held to special privileges this category is a form of apartheid. Nelson Mandela brought about the end of apartheid in Africa and he stands as a shining example for us today. All throughout history there have been instances of apartheid, and I would hope that we feel the higher calling to do away with these at the graduation through effective remedy. Also without the "price neutral revenue", the funding of apartheid would then be on the jurisdiction and the people. With the "compliance alliance" and in light of human rights, we aim to end all forms of discrimination.

Ten. Reparations

To many people there is a form of graduation, great work has been done by the innocence project towards getting people home after wrongful convictions in the courts. There is also the idea of pardons that are given out by the president in the United States, and by the governors of the states. There is also other ideas that are obscure already in place about effective remedy. These are avenues to begin to study in bringing about reparations. I would like to hear about pardons on the News rather than the typical news feed of today. The effective remedy should be the biggest part of pyranade conversation.

So those are the ten stages of "Christ-Help-Us Justice" System. Pray about this and meditate upon it, and consider my ideas of "Rainbow Reparations" in the next section. Remember that this whole section is entitled "Courting." We find when change happens too fast, it does create a wave of opposition, as we found out with the shift of the exiting and entering administrations in America in January of 2017. We want to be both diligent and pragmatic in the appointed times of and prayers for change and transition. In the Book of Ecclesiastes it says, "He makes all things beautiful in his time."

UN BOOK

Section 4

Rainbow Reparations

This is a proposal that I have written;
Rainbow Reparations, Part 1

* Support the new agreement to divide pyranades
into 7 categories with 7 unique responses.
* Reparations in full for all pyranades
* Reassign people in justice system to help all people by new "rainbow" program
* Only RED go to the blue neighborhood named after Troye Sivan's CD for all who
are prisoners inside, and it manifests outside. If they stay more than 6 months then
at 6 months he or she can easily go free (after blue neighborhood is in place)
If at 6 months you can not see a healthy way to integrate person, they
shall be given into a church program of their faith with 10 days access
to research, then they go home. A case worker will be assigned to all
pyranades, and the church will help them decide how to integrate.

Rainbow Reparations, Part 2

• The 7 categories of Rainbow Reparation are; RED for jealousy, ORANGE
for sexuality, YELLOW for drugs, GREEN for financial, BLUE for neurodiverse,
PURPLE for resistance, and PINK for cultural or religious zeal.
• To learn these you learn the reindeer starting down through;
dasher, dancer, prancer, vixion, comet, cupid, and doner.
• RED is the only color that requires, at last resort, coercion. RED
can be taken to the blue neighborhood, for temporary stay, but
eventually the concept in a vibrant generation will go away.
• To free a person safely and healthily is the incentive. A maximum
6 months under RED becomes PURPLE for resistance
These are the only 2 colors that can be requisite in a sane society of forcing
people under obligation. Force looking like and not exceeding taking someone
scared on a roller coaster the first time to try it, or a mother feeding a child
vegetables because she knows that it is good for them, and in their best interest.
• A person is free from the blue neighborhood under PURPLE, where they are under
10 days of guidance supervision where they have access to research and at 10 days
the pyranade if not given housing has no obligation to remain under purple, but to
receive reparations through PURPLE, and the pyranade gets all their money back.
• It is the incentive to quickly more people from RED into
another category of understanding, all other colors have
government run programs to get your reparations in full.
• ORANGE has its own program free of obligation but has help available
under initiative – including supporting the pregnant and sexuality education,
of ethics and morality. ORANGE and BLUE, are brother and sister.
Liberation comes through ORANGE and reparations through BLUE.

- YELLOW has its own program free of obligation, but has help available. There will be "ween centers" for addiction, where a person can ween off a drug at their own pace. Here YELLOW can receive reparations in full, or if they would like reparations in full through BLUE.
- GREEN has its own program that obligates community service to pay restitution to whom it is owed, or by some deal. A financial adviser is given to look after this, open to the pyranade are strategies using government to do this. Then after restitution the reparations left over go to pyranade, and he or she is free of their debt and obligation, at no interest.
- BLUE is a network of mental health given with a case worker at no obligation to the pyranade, also to supply housing, food, water, love and fellowship. No obligation under blue, but government help. Reparations given through BLUE. All members of the city can use this BLUE program.
- PURPLE is resistance, which is easily undone. A person under 10 days obligation with access to research at will and to be in the world at large, but obligated to supervision that is accommodating. Reparations can be liberated through PURPLE, (ORANGE), YELLOW, GREEN, BLUE, and PINK.
- PINK represents those who act out of religious or cultural zeal. This program will provide education on culture and religion, and to bring higher awareness through a local melting pot center. PINK gives accommodations and can get reparations back in full. No obligation in PINK.

Rainbow Reparations, Part 3
- In the transition what it looks like is everyone under obligation is RED, to move to another color would look like a pardon from all obligation, and eventually by the same program reparations in full.
- Transition programs can be to gather large groups of pyranades by number to transfer them into another color, and back into the world at large.
- Lord Jesus be blessed above all.

Here are abstracts on the Rainbow reparations

It's time to invite sanity into our way of understanding sins and quickly rectify them. That there is multiple ways to spell out sin, is not serving the interest of the gestalt whole. Here is an Introduction to the 7 colors of RAINBOW reparations.

RED – Jealousy
As God is named Jealous, human beings have strong emotions towards those they love. This is natural, and we want to help you healthily deal with this natural human emotion.

ORANGE – Sexuality
America is a highly repressive culture so this topic has little clarity. Our cultural understanding of sexuality is not absolute. There are some hyper repressive and some hyper sexed, both are sides to the same coin. We want to come up with a global consciousness on this subject.

YELLOW – Drugs
In our culture we have much drug addiction and irrational beliefs about them. We want to find peaceful clarity and freedom from addiction. A good source is Terrence Mckenna.

GREEN – Financial
In a culture of scarcity, it is logical people will look for a bigger piece. The solution is to work on financial stability and moral and ethical usage for money. We want all to have creative abundance.

BLUE – Neurodiversity
People are very unique in their brains, bodies, and how they use them. We want to celebrate these specializations and channel them in a way that is beneficial for community.

PURPLE – Resistance
In a world of many personalities the lack of a permission slip from some gatekeeper of the world may cause you to have acted out of that diminished place of your eternal worth. We will help you built a bridge over the augmented reality.

PINK – Cultural, Religious, Ethnocentrism
Thanks to Pocahontas and John Smith, the feud between settler and Indian was quelled. Variances in culture create ethnocentric push back. We will communicate your story and incorporate your testimony.

RED

Jealousy

For now all pyranades would be under the category of Red, and a part of the current RED economy. Now what does Red mean in Rainbow Reparations? In Exodus 20 of the Bible Moses is given by God what are known as the "Ten Commandments." And God introduces himself as, "My Name is Jealous." All ten of the commandments follow that theme, that God is jealous for your singular love. Man in the image of God has this characteristic. In the book of Solomon, "The Song of Songs" the love for God to the church, is expressed by the natural pattern of the love of a man for his bride. Thus the nature of love is jealous, and is exploited in many soap operas towards acts of grandeur.

Jared Leto has a band called, 30 Seconds To Mars and he does a wonderful song called, "The Kill." The Kill is about the volatility of finding alignment in relationships. If people knew what Jared Leto did, that the metaphor is the way to liberate language, we would not have the violence expressed today. Violence is not the key to highlight, but the nature of jealousy and how to deal with it.

Jesus says, "If you are angry with a brother in your thoughts, you have already killed him in your heart." There are a lot of people who through jealousy of another, are subject to sin. This would categorize right now all pyranades who have not yet graduated to effective remedy. In the future, any one who is allowed to be taken without consent and put in a temporary timeout in the form of the Blue Neighborhood will be brought in under the category of RED, that is "all sin is one, and priced at zero." I truly believe there is a lot of conflict in the world that is unnecessary. I think we all can begin to forgive and pyranades will start to reflect a society that does not glorify the violence. There shall be training on the way to get a person to deal with jealousy and anger, and an open forum to make reconciliations.

Blue Neighborhood

All people who go to the Blue Neighborhood would go there knowing that it is a place to help them. The whole jurisdiction must decide on a system of relocation of current pyranades, in order to first demolish the current jurisdictional holding center, and gather together to built the Blue Neighborhood. The Blue Neighborhood is an important part of the city as it is the place where the least among us go. That is Jesus talks about the value of the 1 sheep that stray from the other 99. In the Blue Neighborhood there should be a universal church of the city, that is the cities specialization of holistically looking after the people in the city.

The Blue Neighborhood architects should demolish the old form and relocate the pyranades through UN25 systems to temporary housing through the city networks. The Blue Neighborhood should be outdoor, and respect the understanding of natural disasters and watersheds. The mood of the Blue Neighborhood should be meditative and reflective.

There should be Blue houses in an open neighborhood for people to walk around the Blue Neighborhood at will, with a central church in the Center. Local business can come in to put up restaurants that pyranades can work at. Nobody should have to stay under RED in the Blue Neighborhood for longer than 6 months. After 6 months they are then allowed to graduate to PURPLE, and go through a city organization under UN25 to find permanent housing through a case worker. Under incentivism people will be encouraged to with the city resources available, get back on track. The city should take through a program such as Pennsylvania's "Home Rule" keep of all the pyranades to be handled in our local Blue Neighborhood. Each pyranade being "price neutral", they can not be used for the Red market. It should be the city that sees the value in the Blue Neighborhood.

For Troye Sivan, there should be in each Blue Neighborhood a swimming pool. I would like there to be blue speakers on the walk way that the manager of the Blue Neighborhood can chose playlists. There should also be guest housing for guests to stay in the Blue Neighborhood. The idea of the Judge could be outdated. The only reason to keep someone under RED is if they have an active vendetta to hurt somebody. The pyranade is then graduated to first restitution if need be, and then to reparations in full through a program of ORANGE, YELLOW, GREEN, BLUE or PINK. All foundations of the city should be subject to UN audits and I would propose 30 weeks each year, to teach compliance a week for each Declaration article.

Within the city there should be a pyranade graduation program in place, of kind hearts who take the responsibility of the pyranade and their case worker in finding permanent housing. This system of "PURPLE" should be able to handle renovation and even vacation for the pyranades.

So through "Compliance Alliance" and your knowledge of the nexus 30 commandments of all law agreement, if you want you have a tool to push for a Blue Neighborhood in your area. You want to acknowledge the meaning of the Blue Neighborhood as the place in the city for the lost sheep. You then want to prepare a city system where all the pyranades of a jurisdiction can be housed. You then want to use a "Home Rule" like program of your State to get responsibility of all pyranades in your care so as to rehabilitate them within your jurisdiction. You then want to let the city know that you believe in Human Rights, and you are looking for a humane attitude towards pyranades. You organize with all compliant agreements to be able to relocate, demolish the old structure and idea, and gather resources to built the Blue Neighborhood, which is outdoor with blue houses to come and go to, and with a business center, and a place of recreation including a swimming pool. Each Blue Neighborhood built shows that we are progressing the integrity of human rights, for all people.

ORANGE

Sexuality

After God made the animals, he found that Adam was alone. So he created Eve to be a helper for him. So God gave the command, "Therefore a man will leave his mother, and father, and cling to his wife." Later Jesus said, "What man has brought together let no man put asunder." The issue of sexuality has been to many people, a snake in the beautiful garden of Eden. The UN Book acknowledges that sexuality is something we should think of in a positive light, as God used it to populate his world.

Now at times jealousy can express itself through sexuality. In that case, the issue is not the sexuality but the jealousy. I issue ORANGE as a graduation from RED, as there is very little education of the topic. I propose a building in the town that serves as a point of education about questions. Alfred Kinsey grew up into a scientist in a time segment where the topic was so secret, that superstition ruled over the topic. Kinsey presented an open forum to getting some of these questions answered. There is on this topic very varied opinions around the world, in some Islamic cultures women are not suppose to uncover their face in public.

Now let's contrast that to Ancient Greece. Ancient Greece is important, as the American founders got their idea of democracy from Ancient Greece. Founder Thomas Paine came to America saying, "I want to rebuilt Athens." Greece expressed all polarities of relationships and from that integrity built "one person, one vote."

All of the Greek gods had younger boyfriends, and such was the pattern. The Goddess Artemis loved the girl Kallisto. No more famous of these relationships than of Jesus and the Beloved Disciple John. The relationship of a lover and beloved was called the relationship between "erastes" the older, and "eromenos" the younger. We don't recognize these social patterns as acceptable today, but we need to be cognizant that they occur in human nature.

The document "HR2450" I see as a living document pattern that gives the agreementmaker of tomorrow a good starting platform. I express ORANGE as a category of graduation, and a category of learning. This should be a place of expressing views on sexuality through science, morality, ethics, religion, history, anthropology, and ethnocentrism without being motivated by the Red Economy. Know that this is a big topic that needs to be handled with care. Here is the document that does a very good job of creating an agreement about the topic of sexuality.

114th CONGRESS
1st Session

H. R. 2450

To prohibit, as an unfair and deceptive act or practice, commercial sexual orientation conversion therapy, and for other purposes.

IN THE HOUSE OF REPRESENTATIVES

May 19, 2015

Mr. Ted Lieu of California (for himself, Ms. Pelosi, Mrs. Davis of California, Mr. Engel, Mr. Farr, Mr. Peters, Ms. Hahn, Mrs. Watson Coleman, Mr. McDermott, Mr. Blumenauer, Mr. Meeks, Mr. Takano, Mr. Rush, Mr. Welch, Ms. Clarke of New York, Ms. Lee, Ms. Schakowsky, Mr. Pocan, Mrs. Beatty, Ms. Norton, Mr. Grijalva, Mr. Gutiérrez, Mr. Kildee, Ms. DelBene, Mr. Ellison, Mr. Lewis, Mr. Van Hollen, Mr. Quigley, Mr. Higgins, Mr. Sean Patrick Maloney of New York, Mr. Cárdenas, Mr. Schiff, Ms. Clark of Massachusetts, Mr. Ruiz, Ms. Speier, and Mr. Honda) introduced the following bill; which was referred to the Committee on Energy and Commerce

A BILL

To prohibit, as an unfair and deceptive act or practice, commercial sexual orientation conversion therapy, and for other purposes.

Be it enacted by the Senate and House of Representatives of the United States of America in Congress assembled,

SECTION 1. Short title.

This Act may be cited as the "Therapeutic Fraud Prevention Act".

SEC. 2. Findings.

Congress finds that—

(1) being lesbian, gay, bisexual, transgender, or gender nonconforming is not a disorder, disease, illness, deficiency, or shortcoming;

(2) the national community of professionals in education, social work, health, mental health, and counseling has determined that there is no scientifically valid evidence for attempting to prevent a person from being lesbian, gay, bisexual, transgender, or gender nonconforming;

(3) such professionals have determined that there is no evidence that conversion therapy is effective or that an individual's sexual orientation or gender identity can be changed by conversion therapy;

(4) such professionals have also determined that the potential risks of conversion therapy are not only that it is ineffective, but also substantially dangerous to an individuals's mental and physical health, and has been shown to contribute to depression, self-harm, low self-esteem, family rejection, and suicide; and

(5) it is in the interest of the Nation to make sure that lesbian, gay, bisexual, and transgender people and their families are not defrauded by persons seeking to profit by offering this harmful and wholly ineffective therapy.

SEC. 3. Unfair or deceptive acts and practices related to conversion therapy.

(a) Unlawful conduct.—It shall be unlawful for any person to—

(1) provide conversion therapy to any individual if such person receives monetary compensation in exchange for such services; or

(2) advertise for the provision of conversion therapy where such advertising claims—

(A) to change another individual's sexual orientation or gender identity;

(B) to eliminate or reduce sexual or romantic attractions or feelings toward individuals of the same gender; or

(C) that such efforts are harmless or without risk to individuals receiving such therapy.

(b) Violation of rule.—A violation of subsection (a) shall be treated as a violation of a rule defining an unfair or deceptive act or practice prescribed under section 18(a)(1)(B) of the Federal Trade Commission Act (15 U.S.C. 57a(a)(1)(B)).

(c) Powers of Commission.—The Commission shall enforce this section in the same manner, by the same means, and with the same jurisdiction, powers, and duties as though all applicable terms and provisions of the Federal Trade Commission Act (15 U.S.C. 41 et seq.) were incorporated into and made a part of this Act. Any person who violates subsection (a) shall be subject to the penalties and entitled to the privileges and immunities provided in the Federal Trade Commission Act.

SEC. 4. Conversion therapy defined.

The term "conversion therapy"—

(1) means any practices or treatments by any person that seek to change another individual's sexual orientation or gender identity, including efforts to change behaviors or gender expressions, or to eliminate or reduce sexual or romantic attractions or feelings toward individuals of the same gender if such person receives monetary compensation in exchange for such services; and
(2) does not include practices that—
(A) provide assistance to an individual undergoing a gender transition, or
(B) provide acceptance, support, and understanding of clients or facilitation of clients' coping, social support, and identity exploration and development, including sexual orientation-neutral interventions to prevent or address unlawful conduct or unsafe sexual practices, so long as such efforts do not seek to change sexual orientation or gender identity.

SEC. 5. Severability.

If any provision of this Act, or the application of such provision to any person or circumstance, is held to be unconstitutional, the remainder of this Act, and its application to any person or circumstance shall not be affected thereby.

Yellow

drugs

When it comes to the topic of drugs, everyone acknowledges that there is a war on drugs. There has been a war on drugs all of my life. I always had a bad color on the idea of those who were addicted. The first of which is alcohol. The problem with alcohol for the most part is the problem with transportation. If we see alcohol as a transportation issue, we can get rid of the drinking age and the market that benefits from it. Instead the city should be zoned as to have buses that take people to and from the district where alcohol is served. There could even be a hotel in that district to take people who are not ready to go home, to spend the night to sober up. In the 1920s we tried prohibition, and it was a very big failure for human liberty. Many politicians continue to bring this issue to the forefront. But then I found a teacher about the nature of plants in relationship to what we call drugs, and that teacher was Terrence Mckenna. He truly changed my view on the color of what drugs are and I encourage the reader to study his teachings.

Doctors are now starting to see the medicinal value in marijuana in curing ailments. The drug war taught us that views about this plant were irrational. The known "war on drugs" started with FDR but got a big boost through the Nixon Administration. Paramount to any beliefs about the legitimacy of the drug war is its integrity. Below is a quote by Nixon aide Bud Ehrlichman.

"We knew we couldn't make it illegal to be either against the war or black, but by getting the public to associate the hippies with marijuana and blacks with heroin, and then criminalizing both heavily, we could disrupt those communities. We could arrest their leaders, raid their homes, break up their meetings, and vilify them night after night on the evening news. Did we know we were lying about the drugs? Of course we did."

- Nixon Aide, Bud Ehrlichman

That quote is the integrity of the drug war. It is a big failure and it's time to educate ourselves on the subject. Up in Canada instead of making pyranades out of users, drug users are allowed to go to "ween centers" or "harm reduction centers" in order to use in a controlled environment. I purpose under YELLOW that we create these ween centers as a normative in each city. We want to graduate people from RED to YELLOW in terms of getting effective remedy and reparations in full. The use of YELLOW should be voluntary in the city system of reparations. At these centers should be access to doctors who proscribe medical marijuana and doctors who have a holistic understanding about plant chemistry, and the origin of drugs. I agree that addiction is something that can be harmful to a person, but it is something that should be seen as a collective, public health issue rather than one of right or wrong. I would encourage the place to start would be to look at ways of implementing "ween centers" in your area.

Green

financial

When it comes to money there are many varied opinions on what it is and what it is for. Many people look for money to feed not only themselves, but their family. Jesus speaks that we cannot serve God and money. Now our money that we are entrusted with is our stewardship to humanity. I've heard it said that you should not take financial advice from poor people. I think that is good advice, and I am not a financial adviser. I can only advocate that there are systems in place and should be realized through the UN that Social Security be available for "everybody." That is to say that the financial conversation should be a non issue in a functioning high-energy society that works towards progressive implementation of Human Rights virtues.

Now many people use money as a motivator towards wealth and status. I happen to agree that we do want a platform for creativity to flourish. We have to first ask is a person who becomes a pyranade for financial motivation trying to meet basic needs, or for looking for unjust gain. This is how we will be able to understand them. We want to first concentrate on restitution. And the way to deal with a person who acts out of a position of scarcity, is to equip them with a financial adviser per a city system, to help them manage their finances and per necessity, seek out employment, receive supplementary income for a season of unemployment, and provide them with Social Security.

If nobody were to take action, then nothing would get done. We do want people to be educated and active in the community and scientific progress. We do not want to have actions taken from the place of scarcity. Those actions are usually not productive. If you are not enjoying your work, chances are, people are not enjoying the result. One thing I would like to start is to get everybody who is a pyranade Social Security, and in the form of reparations availability to a financial adviser who is working to improve a person and their family's journey towards financial freedom and abundance. We need to realize that scarcity is something solvable. In the category of GREEN pyranades and their andronades will give restitution to whom it is owed through community service work, and reparations for their effective remedy, as well as a financial adviser to continue to manage their life.

Blue

neurodiversity

There are many people who have varied ways of thinking. Dr. Asperger's categorized kids into several intellectual categories and there was a group who did not fit any category and so they were the unlabeled. These kids became known as the Asperger's kids. And the unknown was labeled under the category of Asperger's. Around the same time there was a Dr. Kanner who noticed these anomalies of people who would be self-centered and internalize everything. He called these people Autistic after the Greek "auto" for self, and these people became treated as a class of medical disorder. With Asperger's the distinction was the differences are normal and natural, and with Kanner's Autism group it was seen as something that needed to be cured. There are many theories on why people are different, some of the conditions are more livable than others, and there are varied degrees of this. A more recent movement is to celebrate our differences in a lump sum of all mental conditions as neurodiversity. This concept I advocate and endorse.

Many suffer under discrimination and stigma for reasons that are beyond their control. This is very sad to me. Many people are owed, and all can receive once implemented reparations through the category of BLUE. And there are especially many people in prison who cannot comprehend the acts of cruelty against them. We have come a long way in understanding that each human being has worth and dignity. Each city should have a designated building and reparations through the category of BLUE, and a group of people who are able to help aid a person with a neurodiversity.

In addition these people should have certain helpers to meet their basic needs, and any cause such as finding food, and housing. We want to promote a world where each person is respected for who they are.

Purple

resistance

One of the conditions that a person can graduate to after their 6 months under Rainbow Reparations is the category of PURPLE. Now purple is about a person who acts out of some kind of lack in their life, and from their place of powerlessness they make bad decisions. A person has the right to remain "in the closet." They should not be pushed out of their comfort zone if they do not know what they want or how to express it. If a person is at a place of lack, he will begin to feel resistance that holds his vibration and energy down. A pyranade needs to restore their shine.

The whole Christ-Help-Us Justice system is a form of resistance. As The Declaration of Human Rights is on the virtue of consent, anything where you are forced to do something you do not want to, is going to cause resistance. Then there is also the virtue of going 2 miles, when a person asks to go one. And life is a way of seeking out equilibrium between people, full of give and take.

The way to help with PURPLE is to implement a process towards life centering, and a planning and evaluation of how to get the person hooked up with a lifestyle that is both healthy and productive for the individual. I purpose this process need not take over 10 days, and that is really enough time to heal and "tune" any person with exposure to good influences. A very good place to start with is to have a center for resistance, and anger, and stress that teaches the practice of meditation

Pink

cultural ethnocentrism

A person who looks at the world around them will start with what is familiar to them. As they begin to expand their consciousness they will start to see that not everybody looks or thinks the same way. We start out with a vagrancy in our thinking and we are slow to accept new ideas. Now especially in the concept of religion there is a very varied way of looking at life. The concept of looking at other cultures as inferior to our own, is called ethnocentrism. Much of the many horrors in our world could have been prevented, and future ones can be with a little bit of education. To see the value in other cultures as equal and superior is called xenocentrism. We are moving towards that becoming a reality, where we do not judge others for their differences but learn to embrace other cultures and get along.

With the expansion in the past century the ability for knowledge to spread out of a localized area changes the way we can interact with the world. Even after the 9/11 Terror attacks in America in 2001, our world is so much more able and equip to promote the realization of Human Rights. All the mediums are in place waiting for those inspired in their duty to community to promote a world where these messages could come about.

Think about the story of Pocahontas and John Smith. The word savages turned to love in opposing sides. The idea of knowledge is a very powerful thing. And a lot of extremism is dulled, when the extremist realizes the concept of ethnocentrism. It is a shame many people have lost their life in mass because somebody believed tenaciously in something that was so wrong that they were very ignorant of. If people did not look to fight, but to educate so many things would change. There should be a a center for learning about citizens and especially pyranades who are transgressing cultures and mores that were normal where they came from.

Here is a place to start. There are 3 major religions in the world and they are Islam, Christianity, and Judaism. They are all connected. And they are not meant to be at odds with each other. In the Bible there is the story of Abraham and his wife Sarah and the Lord speaks a prophecy over Abraham that he will have an offspring that will be as many as the stars in the sky. However Sarah his wife is barren. So she tells Abraham to have interrelations with their maid Hagar. And Hagar gives birth to a son named Ishmael. Sarah now resents the maid for fathering a child with her husband and banishes her from the land. Hagar takes her baby Ishmael out in to the wilderness, where God hears her prayer and he tells her to go back home. Ishmael will be a great and blessed nation. And following Ishmael is the story of Islam.

Abraham and Sarah were able to conceive their own child. This child's name was Issac. And from Issac we get his son Jacob, or Israel. Israel gives birth to the 12 sons. The path of the Jews follow Issac and the path of the Muslims follow Ishmael. It is then from the generations of Abraham that are the bloodline that gives birth to Jesus, who is the Messiah of the Jewish people. The fold is then open to be not only a Jew by blood but a Jew by the spirit, to anybody who accepts Christ. Jesus himself was Jewish, and grew up Jewish. The religion of Islam speaks of Jesus. They consider him to be a prophet. These philosophical differences are of great importance to many, yet the approach should be to fellowship over our differences and celebrate that we have many commonalities

There should be a center under PURPLE within each jurisdiction that serves as a melting pot for understanding in the city. It should be run by historians, and have translators so that people of different cultures are welcomed, and integrated into a land where they may need help adjusting.

un BOOK

Section 5

City Accompaniment

In this section I would like to explore the topic of what goes into a healthy city, and create a bit of a blueprint from the UN25 article. I purpose a new vision for the city that matches Jesus teaching of the value of the least among us, or the lost sheep. In Genesis the story was told of the nation of Babylon, whom built a city to heaven. God said, "there is nothing now that they cannot do" and so God confounded their language. I do see a similar potential problem in a Utopia that is linear of all people. We in turn, do not want a one world government or a one world language, but like our America is a melting pot, we do want a world of variety. For this reason, I do champion the entrepreneur and individual uses of liberty in order to grow and function as a city.

Article 25.

> ➤ Everyone has the right to a standard of living adequate for the health and well-being of himself and of his family, including food, clothing, housing, and medical care and necessary social services, and the right to security in the event of unemployment, sickness, disability, widowhood, old age or other lack of livelihood in circumstances beyond his control.
> ➤ Motherhood and childhood are entitled to special care and assistance. All children, whether born in or out of wedlock, shall enjoy the same social protection.

The key word for growth is the concept of jurisdiction. Within a jurisdiction that has 20,000 people, we need to recognize the value of the 20,000ths person. We need not look to the linear monetary system that creates winners and losers, but create degrees of motion, like a circular, cyclic nature that works in natural systems such as the solar system. We need to start to see the lost sheep of the prison within a jurisdiction as the central aspect of it. In turn in a jurisdiction of 20,000 people, all of the 30 commandments of the United Nations should be available to all 20,000 people for the full development of their personality, and the expression within the brotherhood and sisterhood of all people. Our cities can evolve to be as stable as the seasons in a way that each person can have thriving liberty that's not at the expense of another person's abundance.

The city should also have ministry at the central level, or the foundation church. The church should have an outreach to all those in detainment, where all the people of the city can be cared for and understood by people within the city. Today I would picture the central church of a city, to be seen as a place of tithing. This is not to change the way people worship, but add a new gestalt element to the spirituality of a city. In the city people can pray for all the people in the city, including those who are currently in last. In our world we do have a lot of people who we have forgotten. We need a sane strategy towards dealing with this problem. As people begin to see the city as a gestalt system, where they are stewards of all the people within, our way of seeing each other as a brotherhood and sisterhood will start to bare fruit in brand new ways.

Central to the city should be the church of the foundation. Also there should be then the implementation of Compliance Alliance, and the establishing of some form of Rainbow Reparations. I do leave the door open for each city to be creative and unique, in following the principles from the Declaration. I would consider what I call the Blue Neighborhood and the central church, the same place. The spiritual center of the city should be the place where the lost sheep have unconditional shepherds to guide them. So that would be the place to start is to see the person who is last in the city, the spiritual cornerstone of a jurisdiction.

Now each city should have some sort of theme. The theme should fund the city in all aspects, and use the natural progression of the seasons to bring in a seasonal fund for the community. This is seen best in sporting events, how the love of the sport fuels economies. I propose an idea that I call "event stimulus", which is you run one event every year, and you get the whole town involved. The "event stimulus" could serve as a battery of finance flowing in, and flowing out from the public to the private sector and could create an abundance for each person who lives in the jurisdiction.

With event stimulus you have an attraction to draw people into the city, and also to spend their money there. This in turn now creates an idea where each of the 20,000 people in the city have access to creative abundance to live a life free guided by organization.

Now in UN25 there are 16 programs that are spelled out that each city should have as accompaniments. I purpose that the city create a brochure that shows all of the constituents where they can go to get these needs met. Now I again know that variety and differentiation is something that each person wants to do fresh. This blueprint need not be the same exact way practiced in each city, yet each city should use a blueprint of providence of these 16 categories under UN25 as part of "Compliance Alliance."

> ➢ health
> ➢ well-being
> ➢ family
> ➢ food
> ➢ clothing
> ➢ housing
> ➢ medical care
> ➢ social services
> ➢ unemployment
> ➢ sickness
> ➢ disability
> ➢ widowhood
> ➢ old age
> ➢ lack of livelihood
> ➢ motherhood
> ➢ childhood

Now there is probably already motion on all of these topics within a city. It would be really good for the purposes of Human Rights to organize these so that there is a directory of such dealing with all of these categories. There should be such at every community event a place where you can find out where to go in finding people to aid you in any of these categories. I would suggest having a glyph for each of these UN25 accompaniments that match nicely with fulfilling the basic needs at the bottom of Abraham Maslow's "Hierarchy of Needs." When the basic needs are met, a person can begin to pursue more ascended aspirations towards actualization.

To built the city in a way that is easily accessible is something that is going to take the gifts of all of the people in the city, and their ability to work together. It is a good thing to have a city that is conscious of all the people who live in it, and a city that can grow together. I purpose creating a "Compliance Alliance" within your city, that specializes in maintaining the virtues of the 30 articles of the Declaration of Human Rights. As your compliance alliance grows there should be 30 weeks out of the 52 week year, where the 30 commandments, or articles are highlighted in a city.

Here is my proposal:

In a jurisdiction of 20,000 people, we implement a Compliance Alliance for all 20,000 people. We will bring humanity to the place of jurisdiction through the 30 commandments, each celebrated at 1 week of the year. Central to the city is a central place that looks out for the spiritual needs of all 20,000 people starting with the pyranades. You begin to gradually gain momentum of the virtues of the Declaration of Human Rights and start to seek reparations for people, in humanizing the system. It starts with a commitment to the spiritual health and well-being of all people.

Now the jurisdiction needs some central form of government, which we already have in place. There needs to be citizen participation in order to promote the values of the United Nations Declaration. You now have a system of asking, where all people are equals in participation. And when you have a city gestalt system, you can now begin to implement the 16 UN25 accompaniments which I will describe some of my ideas about how to work with them.

Health Audits

In the center for city government there should be a place to do "Health Audits" that you can express how you are feeling. These should be available within the foundations and each person's audits should go to the central City where it can be read by Compliance Alliance in the public capacity. Everyone should have access to these health audits, and from these writings any one in the City can be connected with the powers that can bring health changes.

Well-being Audits

In addition to "Health Audits" there should be a second forum for "Well-Being Audits" where a person can express their Well-being in a way that can be reviewed by the citizens of the community. To achieve Well-being is a moving target in life, even if a person is lonely, there should be people who are to gather for that purpose of furthering their role in the community through care for their well-being.

Family Audits

Sometimes a person can not or does not want to speak directly for themselves, and they may want to communicate through a family audit. The idea of the andronade can speak for pyranades. In addition through the family audit, families can have asking that might promote their cause within and through community. These family audits can be reviewed at the central place of city government like the audits for health and well-being.

Food

Under UN25 in the Declaration, food is listed as a human right. This means that all people should have adequate food. But the thing about food is that it must be planted and harvested. Our law agreement is in place, we just need to find the right procedure. Food should be something that fuels the economy and the body. A distribution system should be in place where by the graduated system of finances, those who have more money and can shop, pay for food in a graduated way through the market that supports their growing lifestyle. At the same time, such a distribution system should be in place where the city provides ways of making sure that each person is fed. Money does not grow in nature, but food does. We have more than enough resources to accomplish this ends, that all people are fed, we just need to put this into practice. There should be places for provided meals in the city in addition to the food that is on the market. This writing supports a graduated private sector. Such places for meals should be promoted by the city so that all people who are hungry, can eat.

Clothing

It is a human right that each person should be provided adequate clothing. It is good that there are stores where you can decorate yourself in the fashions of your hearts desire. There should be places where clothing can be provided for those who have none, including in the foundations. A list of places to get clothing, and places to learn how to make clothing, should be provided in a city brochure so all people in the jurisdiction can be clothed.

Housing

Under the UN25 every human body should have a home. This is something that we can work on within the jurisdiction of the city. The first place to figure out how to house all the people in a jurisdiction. We allow the market to work but at the same time, we have buildings and a plan to relocate all pyranades in the pursuit of building the central church and the new Blue Neighborhood. So the plan for housing should be that each city be incentivized and created such that there is a home for all people. And the home should be adequate. This does take some knowledge, some training, some work and some time. It should however be the virtue of the city, to recognize that housing under our law agreement is listed as a human right. In redesigning cities there should be space provided for the housing needs of all people.

Medical Care

The providence of Medical Care should be the pursuit of some building in the city. There can be multiple medical care providers to create competition, but there should be concern for the medical condition of all people within the jurisdiction. In the brochure of the city, there should be listed the knowledge of how to get medical care.

Social Services

Many social services should be available for the socialization of the individual. Such social services should include transportation that gets people around the city. We would want from the spiritual center of the city, to project outward a system of transportation and a system of community where each person is encouraged to find their full development.

Unemployment

Each person who is not employed who seeks finances should be granted accrual of unemployment. This is also a place that should provide options of growth and employment to the people. Under UN25 this is an accompaniment that each person should have access to. If a person is not working, they should have some way of funding their basic needs.

Sickness

Within the city there should be a program dealing with people who are sick and people who are sad. If a person is sick and they need extra financing to cover that, then there can be accrual through some sort of insurance or compensation for a person who is dealing with a medical problem.

Disability

If a person has a disability, then they should have a program that is tailored to their needs dealing with the disability. In the city there should be a place where people who are disabled can receive benefits and life tools to function healthily within the community.

Widowhood

If a person is left behind by a husband or wife, the city should provide aid in dealing with all the things that arise from losing a loved one. The city should provide an outreach to widows including help with their financing, so they are able to go on after loss.

Old Age

When a person grows into old age, they will encounter new needs with the aging process. The city should provide care for those who are transitioning into the phase of their life where they have special needs. The city program should be tailored to accommodating the needs of people who are aging, and provide resources to them through nursing homes.

Lack of Livelihood

In addition to unemployment, the United Nations Declaration of Human Rights gives ear to the category of lack of livelihood. Each city should have such a providence for people who are without a current direction or way of comprehension. The lack of livelihood should be a program that specializes in inspiring people and in finding them direction.

Motherhood

What would we do without our mothers? Motherhood is a very special process and the city should acknowledge that the mothers, and to be mothers have specialized needs with bringing the baby into the world, keeping them healthy, and providing for them. There should be a program where mothers have a sense of community that help them in raising their child.

Childhood

Children have many needs associated with them. Mothers and fathers have a lot of questions, and so do kids. There should be within the city, a program that specializes in the care of children. In addition to the providing of free education there should be places to send the kids when the parents have to work.

These are 16 basic categories spelled out in the United Nations that can make the body of a city flow and function. I like to picture these as 16 buildings within the city, where you can take your concerns on these subjects, and you can have adequate providence of these basic life needs, and pursue the life of your dreams and desires. This was the vision of 1948 and this is the realization that I see today.

UN BOOK

Section 6

Customization

This section is to keep your notes about the 30 commandments of the United Nations Declaration of Human Rights.

Preamble

Whereas recognition of the inherent dignity and of the equal and inalienable rights of all members of the human family is the foundation of freedom, justice and peace in the world,

Whereas disregard and contempt for human rights have resulted in barbarous acts which have outraged the conscience of mankind, and the advent of a world in which human beings shall enjoy freedom of speech and belief and freedom from fear and want has been proclaimed as the highest aspiration of the common people,

Whereas it is essential, if man is not to be compelled to have recourse, as a last resort, to rebellion against tyranny and oppression, that human rights should be protected by the rule of law,

Whereas it is essential to promote the development of friendly relations between nations,

Whereas the peoples of the United Nations have in the Charter reaffirmed their faith in fundamental human rights, in the dignity and worth of the human person and in the equal rights of men and women and have determined to promote social progress and better standards of life in larger freedom,

Whereas Member States have pledged themselves to achieve, in co-operation with the United Nations, the promotion of universal respect for and observance of human rights and fundamental freedoms,

Whereas a common understanding of these rights and freedoms is of the greatest importance for the full realization of this pledge,

Now, Therefore THE GENERAL ASSEMBLY proclaims THIS UNIVERSAL DECLARATION OF HUMAN RIGHTS as a common standard of achievement for all peoples and all nations, to the end that every individual and every organ of society, keeping this Declaration constantly in mind, shall strive by teaching and education to promote respect for these rights and freedoms and by progressive measures, national and international, to secure their universal and effective recognition and observance, both among the peoples of Member States themselves and among the peoples of territories under their jurisdiction.

Article 1

All human beings are born free and equal in dignity and rights. They are endowed with reason and conscience and should act towards one another in a spirit of brotherhood.

Article 2

Everyone is entitled to all rights and freedoms set forth in this Declaration, without distinction of any kind, such as race, colour, sex, language, religion, political or other opinion, national or social origin, property, birth or other status.

Furthermore, no distinction shall be made on the basis of the political, jurisdictional or international status of the country or territory to which a person belongs, whether it be independent, trust, non-self-governing or under any other limitation of sovereignty.

Article 3

Everyone has the right to life, liberty, and security of person.

Article 4

No one shall be held in slavery or servitude; slavery and the slave trade shall be prohibited in all their forms.

Article 5

No one shall be subjected to torture or to cruel, inhuman or degrading treatment or punishment.

Article 6

Everyone has the right to recognition everywhere as a person before the law.

Article 7

All are equal before the law and are entitled without discrimination to equal protection of the law. All are entitled to equal protection against any discrimination in violation of this Declaration and against any incitement to such discrimination.

Article 8

Everyone has the right to an effective remedy by the competent national tribunals for acts violating the fundamental rights granted him by the constitution of by law.

Article 9

No one shall be subjected to arbitrary arrest, detention, or exile.

Article 10

Everyone is entitled in full equality to a fair and public hearing by an independent and impartial tribunal, in the determination of his rights and obligations of any criminal charges against him.

Article 11

- ➤ Everyone charged with a penal offence has the right to be presumed innocent until proved guilty according to the law in a public trial at which he has had all guarantees necessary for his defence.
- ➤ No one shall be held guilty of any penal offence on account of any act or omission which did not constitute a penal offence, under national or international law, at the time when it was committed. Nor shall a heavier penalty be imposed than the one that was applicable at the time the penal offence was committed.

Article 12

No one shall be subjected to arbitrary interference with his privacy, family, home or correspondence, nor to attacks upon his honour and reputation. Everyone has the right to the protection of the law against such interference or attacks.

Article 13

> Everyone has the right to freedom of movement and residence within the borders of each State.
> Everyone has the right to leave any country, including his own, and to return to his country

Article 14

> ➢ Everyone has the right to seek and to enjoy in other countries asylum from persecution.
> ➢ This right may not be invoked in the case of prosecutions genuinely arising from non-political crimes or from acts contrary to the purposes and principles of the United Nations.

Article 15

➢ Everyone has the right to a nationality.
➢ No one shall be arbitrarily deprived of his nationality nor denied the right to change nationality.

Article 16

- ➤ Men and women of full age, without any limitation due to race, nationality or religion, have the right to marry and to found a family. They are entitled to equal rights as to marriage, during marriage and at its dissolution.
- ➤ Marriage shall be entered into only with the free and full consent of the intending spouses.
- ➤ The family is the natural and fundamental group unit of society and is entitled to protection by society and the State.

Article 17

➤ Everyone has the right to own property alone as well as in association with others.
➤ No one shall be arbitrarily deprived of his property.

Article 18

Everyone has the right to freedom of thought, conscience and religion; this right includes freedom to change his religion or belief, and freedom, either alone or in community with others and in public or private, to manifest his religion or belief in teaching, practice, worship, and observance.

Article 19

Everyone has the right to freedom of opinion and expression; this right includes freedom to hold opinions without interference and to seek, receive and impart information and ideas through any media and regardless of frontiers.

Article
20

> ➢ Everyone has the right to freedom of peaceful assembly and association.
> ➢ No one may be compelled to belong to an association

Article 21

- ➢ Everyone has the right to take part in the government of his country, directly or through freely chosen representatives.
- ➢ Everyone has the right to equal access to public service in his country.
- ➢ The will of the people shall be the basis of the authority of government; this will shall be expressed in periodic and genuine elections which shall be by universal and equal suffrage and shall be held by secret vote or by equivalent free voting procedures.

Article 22

Everyone, as a member of society, has the right to social security and is entitled to realization, through national effort and international co-operation and in accordance with the organization and resources of each State, of the economic, social and cultural rights indispensable for his dignity and the free development of his personality.

Article 23

➢ Everyone has the right to work, to free choice of employment, to just and favourable conditions of work and to protection against unemployment.

➢ Everyone, without any discrimination, has the right to equal pay for equal work.

➢ Everyone who works has the right to just and favourable remuneration ensuring for himself and his family an existence worthy of human dignity, and supplemented, if necessary, by other means of social protection.

➢ Everyone has the right to form and to join trade unions for the protection of his interests.

Article 24

Everyone has the right to rest and leisure, including reasonable limitation of working hours and periodic holidays with pay.

Article
25

➤ Everyone has the right to a standard of living adequate for the health and well-being of himself and of his family, including food, clothing, housing, and medical care and necessary social services, and the right to security in the event of unemployment, sickness, disability, widowhood, old age or other lack of livelihood in circumstances beyond his control.

➤ Motherhood and childhood are entitled to special care and assistance. All children, whether born in or out of wedlock, shall enjoy the same social protection.

Article 26

- Everyone has the right to education. Education shall be free, at least in the elementary and fundamental stages. Elementary education shall be compulsory. Technical and professional education shall be made generally available and higher education shall be equally accessible to all on the basis of merit.
- Education shall be directed to the full development of the human personality and to the strengthening of respect for human rights and fundamental freedoms. It shall further the activities of the United Nations for the maintenance of peace.
- Parents have a prior right to choose the kind of education that shall be given to their children

Article 27

- ➢ Everyone has the right freely to participate in the cultural life of the community, to enjoy the arts and to share in scientific advancement and its benefits.
- ➢ Everyone has the right to the protection of the moral and material interests resulting from any scientific, literary or artistic production of which he the author.

Article 28

Everyone is entitled to a social and international order in which the rights and freedoms set forth in this Declaration can be fully realized.

Article 29

- ➢ Everyone has duties to the community in which alone the free and full development of his personality is possible.
- ➢ In the exercise of his rights and freedoms, everyone shall be subject only to such limitations as are determined by law solely for the purpose of securing due recognition and respect for the rights and freedoms of others and of meeting the just requirements of morality, public order, and the general welfare in a democratic society.
- ➢ These rights and freedoms may in no case be exercised contrary to the purposes and principles of the United Nations.

Article 30

Nothing in this Declaration may be interpreted as implying for any State, group, or person any right to engage in any activity or to perform any act aimed at the destruction of any of the rights and freedoms set forth herein.

The Full Declaration of Human Rights

Preamble

Whereas recognition of the inherent dignity and of the equal and inalienable rights of all members of the human family is the foundation of freedom, justice and peace in the world,

Whereas disregard and contempt for human rights have resulted in barbarous acts which have outraged the conscience of mankind, and the advent of a world in which human beings shall enjoy freedom of speech and belief and freedom from fear and want has been proclaimed as the highest aspiration of the common people,

Whereas it is essential, if man is not to be compelled to have recourse, as a last resort, to rebellion against tyranny and oppression, that human rights should be protected by the rule of law,

Whereas it is essential to promote the development of friendly relations between nations,

Whereas the peoples of the United Nations have in the Charter reaffirmed their faith in fundamental human rights, in the dignity and worth of the human person and in the equal rights of men and women and have determined to promote social progress and better standards of life in larger freedom,

Whereas Member States have pledged themselves to achieve, in co-operation with the United Nations, the promotion of universal respect for and observance of human rights and fundamental freedoms,

Whereas a common understanding of these rights and freedoms is of the greatest importance for the full realization of this pledge,

Now, Therefore THE GENERAL ASSEMBLY proclaims THIS UNIVERSAL DECLARATION OF HUMAN RIGHTS as a common standard of achievement for all peoples and all nations, to the end that every individual and every organ of society, keeping this Declaration constantly in mind, shall strive by teaching and education to promote respect for these rights and freedoms and by progressive measures, national and international, to secure their universal and effective recognition and observance, both among the peoples of Member States themselves and among the peoples of territories under their jurisdiction.

Article 1.
All human beings are born free and equal in dignity and rights. They are endowed with reason and conscience and should act towards one another in a spirit of brotherhood.

Article 2.

Everyone is entitled to all the rights and freedoms set forth in this Declaration, without distinction of any kind, such as race, colour, sex, language, religion, political or other opinion, national or social origin, property, birth or other status. Furthermore, no distinction shall be made on the basis of the political, jurisdictional or international status of the country or territory to which a person belongs, whether it be independent, trust, non-self-governing or under any other limitation of sovereignty.

Article 3.

Everyone has the right to life, liberty and security of person.

Article 4.

No one shall be held in slavery or servitude; slavery and the slave trade shall be prohibited in all their forms.

Article 5.

No one shall be subjected to torture or to cruel, inhuman or degrading treatment or punishment.

Article 6.

Everyone has the right to recognition everywhere as a person before the law.

Article 7.

All are equal before the law and are entitled without any discrimination to equal protection of the law. All are entitled to equal protection against any discrimination in violation of this Declaration and against any incitement to such discrimination.

Article 8.

Everyone has the right to an effective remedy by the competent national tribunals for acts violating the fundamental rights granted him by the constitution or by law.

Article 9.

No one shall be subjected to arbitrary arrest, detention or exile.

Article 10.

Everyone is entitled in full equality to a fair and public hearing by an independent and impartial tribunal, in the determination of his rights and obligations and of any criminal charge against him.

Article 11.

(1) Everyone charged with a penal offence has the right to be presumed innocent until proved guilty according to law in a public trial at which he has had all the guarantees necessary for his defence.

(2) No one shall be held guilty of any penal offence on account of any act or omission which did not constitute a penal offence, under national or international law, at the time when it was committed. Nor shall a heavier penalty be imposed than the one that was applicable at the time the penal offence was committed.

Article 12.
No one shall be subjected to arbitrary interference with his privacy, family, home or correspondence, nor to attacks upon his honour and reputation. Everyone has the right to the protection of the law against such interference or attacks.

Article 13.
(1) Everyone has the right to freedom of movement and residence within the borders of each state.
(2) Everyone has the right to leave any country, including his own, and to return to his country.

Article 14.
(1) Everyone has the right to seek and to enjoy in other countries asylum from persecution.
(2) This right may not be invoked in the case of prosecutions genuinely arising from non-political crimes or from acts contrary to the purposes and principles of the United Nations.

Article 15.
(1) Everyone has the right to a nationality.
(2) No one shall be arbitrarily deprived of his nationality nor denied the right to change his nationality.

Article 16.
(1) Men and women of full age, without any limitation due to race, nationality or religion, have the right to marry and to found a family. They are entitled to equal rights as to marriage, during marriage and at its dissolution.
(2) Marriage shall be entered into only with the free and full consent of the intending spouses.
(3) The family is the natural and fundamental group unit of society and is entitled to protection by society and the State.

Article 17.
(1) Everyone has the right to own property alone as well as in association with others.
(2) No one shall be arbitrarily deprived of his property.

Article 18.
Everyone has the right to freedom of thought, conscience and religion; this right includes freedom to change his religion or belief, and freedom, either alone or in community with others and in public or private, to manifest his religion or belief in teaching, practice, worship and observance.

Article 19.
Everyone has the right to freedom of opinion and expression; this right includes freedom to hold opinions without interference and to seek, receive and impart information and ideas through any media and regardless of frontiers.

Article 20.
(1) Everyone has the right to freedom of peaceful assembly and association.
(2) No one may be compelled to belong to an association.

Article 21.
(1) Everyone has the right to take part in the government of his country, directly or through freely chosen representatives.
(2) Everyone has the right of equal access to public service in his country.
(3) The will of the people shall be the basis of the authority of government; this will shall be expressed in periodic and genuine elections which shall be by universal and equal suffrage and shall be held by secret vote or by equivalent free voting procedures.

Article 22.
Everyone, as a member of society, has the right to social security and is entitled to realization, through national effort and international co-operation and in accordance with the organization and resources of each State, of the economic, social and cultural rights indispensable for his dignity and the free development of his personality.

Article 23.
(1) Everyone has the right to work, to free choice of employment, to just and favourable conditions of work and to protection against unemployment.
(2) Everyone, without any discrimination, has the right to equal pay for equal work.
(3) Everyone who works has the right to just and favourable remuneration ensuring for himself and his family an existence worthy of human dignity, and supplemented, if necessary, by other means of social protection.
(4) Everyone has the right to form and to join trade unions for the protection of his interests.

Article 24.
Everyone has the right to rest and leisure, including reasonable limitation of working hours and periodic holidays with pay.

Article 25.
(1) Everyone has the right to a standard of living adequate for the health and well-being of himself and of his family, including food, clothing, housing and medical care and necessary social services, and the right to security in the event of unemployment, sickness, disability, widowhood, old age or other lack of livelihood in circumstances beyond his control.
(2) Motherhood and childhood are entitled to special care and assistance. All children, whether born in or out of wedlock, shall enjoy the same social protection.

Article 26.

(1) Everyone has the right to education. Education shall be free, at least in the elementary and fundamental stages. Elementary education shall be compulsory. Technical and professional education shall be made generally available and higher education shall be equally accessible to all on the basis of merit.

(2) Education shall be directed to the full development of the human personality and to the strengthening of respect for human rights and fundamental freedoms. It shall promote understanding, tolerance and friendship among all nations, racial or religious groups, and shall further the activities of the United Nations for the maintenance of peace.

(3) Parents have a prior right to choose the kind of education that shall be given to their children.

Article 27.

(1) Everyone has the right freely to participate in the cultural life of the community, to enjoy the arts and to share in scientific advancement and its benefits.

(2) Everyone has the right to the protection of the moral and material interests resulting from any scientific, literary or artistic production of which he is the author.

Article 28.

Everyone is entitled to a social and international order in which the rights and freedoms set forth in this Declaration can be fully realized.

Article 29.

(1) Everyone has duties to the community in which alone the free and full development of his personality is possible.

(2) In the exercise of his rights and freedoms, everyone shall be subject only to such limitations as are determined by law solely for the purpose of securing due recognition and respect for the rights and freedoms of others and of meeting the just requirements of morality, public order and the general welfare in a democratic society.

(3) These rights and freedoms may in no case be exercised contrary to the purposes and principles of the United Nations.

Article 30.

Nothing in this Declaration may be interpreted as implying for any State, group or person any right to engage in any activity or to perform any act aimed at the destruction of any of the rights and freedoms set forth herein.

God Bless You

Printed in the United States
By Bookmasters